D1454244

The Concept of the Social

The Concept of the Social

Scepticism, Idleness and Utopia

Malcolm Bull

VERSO

London • New York

First published by Verso 2021
© Malcolm Bull 2021

Chapter 2. *New Left Review* 45, May–June 2007; 3. *New Left Review* 35,
Sept–Oct 2005; 4. *New Left Review* 40, July–Aug 2006; 5. *New Left Review*
100, July–Aug 2016; 6. Katrina Forrester and Sophie Smith, eds, *Nature,
Action and the Future*, Cambridge 2018

1 3 5 7 9 10 8 6 4 2

Verso
UK: 6 Meard Street, London W1F 0EG
US: 20 Jay Street, Suite 1010, Brooklyn, NY 11201
versobooks.com

Verso is the imprint of New Left Books

ISBN-13: 978-1-84467-293-6
ISBN-13: 978-1-83976-430-1 (US EBK)
ISBN-13: (UK EBK)

British Library Cataloguing in Publication Data
A catalogue record for this book is available from the British Library

Library of Congress Cataloging-in-Publication Data
A catalog record for this book is available from the Library of Congress

Contents

Acknowledgements

This book has been some time in the making, and the essays it contains have been shaped by many hands other than my own. Several were originally presented as invited papers: chapter 4 at a workshop on 'Democracy, Markets and War' at the United Nations in New York; chapter 5 at a conference on 'Rethinking Crowds' at Istanbul Bilgi University; and chapter 6 at the Philomathia Conference on Political Thought and the Environment at Cambridge. I am very grateful to the late Istvan Hont, Zeynep Koçak, Katrina Forrester and Sophie Smith for the invitations, and to the other participants in these events for their questions and comments. Chapters 2 to 5 were previously published in *New Left Review*, where I am especially indebted to the editor, Susan Watkins. Chapter 6 appeared in *Nature, Action and the Future*, published by Cambridge University Press and edited by Katrina Forrester and Sophie Smith.

I would particularly like to thank Steven Lukes and Amia Srinivasan for their comments on chapter 1, Christopher

Brooke for comments on chapter 7, and Perry Anderson, who read the entire manuscript. At Verso, it has been a pleasure to work with a succession of editors: Tom Penn, Leo Hollis and Tom Hazeldine (who finally saw the book to press). My greatest debt is, as always, to Jill Foulston.

Introduction

The starting point for this book is the uncertainty and incompleteness of our knowledge, and our knowledge of politics in particular. It does not set out to make that knowledge any more secure, but rather to explore ways in which uncertainty might contribute to, rather than impede, our collective emancipation.

Progressive politics often seems wedded to the idea that knowledge and knowledge-based action provide the only route to a utopian future. But experience suggests that there's more that we don't know than we do, and that while some outcomes are the intended consequences of our actions the majority are not. And that even if that's not the case in our most immediate experience and actions, it becomes increasingly true as the frame of reference expands. It follows from this that a mild to moderate degree of scepticism is probably warranted when it comes to questions about the ultimate goals of politics and how to achieve them.

From such seemingly modest observations, powerful currents of anti-utopian thought were developed in the mid-twentieth century by Oakeshott and Hayek among others. Those ideas have transformed our world. This book is a response to these thinkers, not in the sense that it engages directly with their arguments, but in that it starts from similar premisses and heads in another direction. On the one hand, it assumes that what we need to be freed from is not our ignorance, but what we think we know already; on the other, it accepts that our world is made through collective action. It therefore argues that collective emancipation is possible, and that it is achieved through the unmaking of the world.

The name that is given to this utopian possibility is 'the social'. The term is taken from Hannah Arendt who, like many other critics of modernity, noticed that the world was in the process of being unmade without anyone having intended to dismantle it. In what follows, the social is taken not as a symptom of political and cultural decline, but rather as an intimation of utopian possibility. If we need to free ourselves from the things that we ourselves have made, we may yet achieve emancipation through the unintended consequences of our own (in)action. Any specifiable state of the world contains the promise of a greater degree of spontaneous disorder, and a degree of scepticism about politics suggests we might allow ourselves to relax enough to achieve it. Like many works of political theory, this book is much concerned with nature and the state. But rather than being an argument about how the political state can arise from the state of nature, it is concerned with the reverse dynamic: how the political state can be returned to nature.

Antarctic explorers classify their journeys according to whether they are *expeditions* (to the South Pole and back), *crossings* (from one side to the other), or *circumnavigations* (around the pole), and also whether they are *full* (e.g., starting at the coast and returning to it) or *partial* (starting and/or ending somewhere further inland). It's a classification system that can easily be applied to intellectual exploration as well. And in these terms, *The Concept of the Social* is not a full expedition in that it does not start from some notionally neutral premiss outside its subject matter and keep on arguing until it reaches its goal. Instead, it offers a series of overlapping and intersecting paths across the same territory. Some are circumnavigations, circling the pole without reaching it. Most are partial crossings, picking up a line of argument, heading directly south and not stopping until some way beyond the pole itself. And some are reverse crossings, which begin where someone else has stopped and retrace their steps in the opposite direction. But as in all polar explorations, each of these paths crosses or circles around the same point, and all share the same orientation and purpose.

If traced on a map, these paths might look something like a net, not perhaps one so tightly drawn as to trap the elusive concept of the social, but maybe one with enough meshing to retain it for a while before it slips away. The opening chapter draws on social ontology to argue that scepticism has serious yet positive consequences for politics, and that a politics of scepticism can unmake the world and bring human and non-human nature into alignment. That alignment is potentially to be found in the space that

Arendt designates as 'the social', and chapter 2, 'Vectors of the Biopolitical', sketches the routes through which the political and the natural might converge there. The following three chapters are concerned more specifically with questions of political agency and explore the relationship between the political and the social, state and society. In particular, they highlight ways in which unintended consequences may create, not a form of spontaneous order, but the kind of spontaneous disorder that Hegel identified with 'civil society' and Machiavelli with 'corruption', and which turns out to be potentially far healthier than either allows. Machiavelli suggests that one of the things that leads to corruption is idleness, and in 'Slack' it is possible to see this argument unfold in the debate about unused resources in twentieth-century environmentalism. The final chapter argues that increasing the unused potential of the human race may be the best route to a natural cosmopolitanism.

1

The Concept of the Social

Is Scepticism Possible?

What can we know to be true? What is the right way to
live? What sort of society is best?

These are questions that might occur to anyone. But
we may well find that we do not have good answers and
doubt that convincing answers even exist. It is so easy to
be over-confident. Just think of all the ways the world has
made sense to people in the past and how wrong they have
been. And yet, if life is to go on, we have to act as though
we know what is true, and what is right, and what is for the
best. But how to proceed, if we don't know which foot to
put forward, or whether we have feet at all?

These questions have been around forever, and they will
probably never go away. People who admit they do not
know the answers are called sceptics. The Greek philosopher Pyrrho is considered to be the founder of scepticism.
He is said to have maintained that 'things are equally indifferent, unmeasurable and inarbitrable' and that 'nothing is

honourable or base, or just and unjust, and that likewise in all cases nothing exists in truth; and that convention and habit are the basis of everything that men do'. In these circumstances he thought 'suspension of judgement' the only appropriate response.[1]

This might seem to offer a good default position on everything, but in practice there are some difficulties.[2] Pyrrho tried to follow the principles of scepticism in his daily life. But he wasn't always successful, and when criticised for being scared by a dog he had to admit 'it was difficult to strip [himself] completely of being human'.[3] And that's exactly the problem. You can maintain that the external world may or may not exist, and that even if it does it is a matter of indifference to you, but when you are bitten by a dog it still hurts, and you shrink the next time a dog comes towards you. Scepticism about the world is all very well until the world bites us back.

Pyrrhonism sought to establish that for any proposition, the arguments for and against it are equally balanced, equipollent. This rationally leads to suspension of judgement or belief, because there is no reason to favour one alternative rather than another, and being indifferent between alternatives produces tranquillity.[4] That's the theory, but in everyday life the sceptic soon runs into what is known as the apraxia challenge: if everything is a matter of indifference, then no one has any reason to do one thing rather than another, and so they will eventually die of indecision like Buridan's ass. Either the sceptic is inconsistent in their scepticism, as Pyrrho acknowledged himself to be with the dog, or else the sceptic is committed to a way of life that is terminally inactive, at best the life of a plant or an animal rather than a human being.[5]

Although this objection to scepticism was obvious from the start, it was David Hume who stated it most eloquently. If everyone were to live like that, 'all discourse and all action would immediately cease; and men would remain in a total lethargy until their miserable lives came to an end through lack of food, drink and shelter'. Hume's point is not that Pyrrhonism will die out, but that its survival tells us something about what is wrong with it:

> The great subverter of Pyrrhonism, or the excessive principles of scepticism, is action, and employment, and the occupations of common life. These principles may flourish and triumph in the schools; where it is, indeed, difficult, if not impossible, to refute them. But as soon as they leave the shade, and by the presence of the real objects, which actuate our passions and sentiments, are put in opposition to the more powerful principles of our nature, they vanish like smoke and leave the most determined sceptic in the same condition as other mortals.[6]

On this view, scepticism is in a sense both justified and impossible: 'Philosophy would render us entirely Pyrrhonian', but 'Nature, by an absolute and uncontrollable necessity, *makes* us judge as well as breathe and feel'.[7]

For Hume, Pyrrhonism, like other philosophies, is too ready to assume that our actions are, or at least ought to be, guided by reason at all times. That is looking in the wrong place for the sources of our motivation. The world itself never provides adequate motivation for our choices. It is not the weighing of external evidence but internal desire that determines judgement and action: 'Nothing can oppose or retard the impulse of passion, but a contrary impulse.'[8] Indeed, as Bernard Williams later argued, perhaps the very idea of a (purely) external reason is incoherent because there is no account of what is involved in accepting an external reason that does not invoke internal motivation.[9]

However, as John Searle has pointed out, the idea that 'a rational act can only be motivated by a desire' is absurd because it assumes that in the absence of 'a desire, broadly construed, then and there', an agent has no reason for action.[10] Whereas in everyday life knowing some external fact about the world, such as the fact that you've ordered a drink at a café and then drunk it, provides a rationally compelling reason for action: namely, paying the bill. In examples like this, an undertaking creates an obligation that provides a reason for action quite independent of any other motivation.

The reason Searle thinks there are external reasons for action is that some facts are social facts rather than natural or 'brute' facts. Many facts about the world exist independently of language or any other institution; these are brute facts (e.g., about mountains and particles), whereas others are social facts that require human institutions in order to exist (e.g., the fact that Elizabeth II is Queen of England).[11] In terms of this distinction, that you have ordered a drink is a social fact, because although liquids are natural entities, placing an order is a social fact. The reason social facts do not disappear with our motivations is that they are facts. It is no good saying that you have doubts about the practice of paying for drinks; if you've ordered a drink, your obligation to pay for it is a social fact.

If we accept Searle's argument here, then it unexpectedly reopens the question of the feasibility of scepticism from another angle. There are certainly good arguments against scepticism, but they may be less effective against some forms of scepticism than others. The strongest argument against scepticism is that no one (i.e., no individual) can live as a sceptic, because they will run into brute facts and real-world choices. But what about political scepticism? Here, above all, Searle's point seems relevant. Things like states and borders and laws are all social facts. And although individuals cannot remake social facts, societies can. It makes no difference whether King Canute or the whole of his society fails to acknowledge brute facts like the existence of tides, but it will matter a lot if Canute's subjects refuse to acknowledge the existence of the monarchy.

In politics, external reasons are always involved because politics deals with social rather than natural facts, and social facts, even if created from internal motivations, may then provide external reasons for action. Does that mean political scepticism is impossible, since, while someone may rationally doubt the existence of one version of the world, they are simultaneously constructing another one? Not necessarily, because the social world is made; so, rather than doubting it, you can make less of it. A social fact cannot be wished or doubted away by any individual, but it can potentially be modified, or an exception made, by the same social processes through which it came into existence in the first place.

This argument suggests a rather different set of possibilities to consider when it comes to scepticism. Rather than conceiving of the sceptic as an individual faced with the intractability of brute facts and the unavoidability of moral agency, we should perhaps think instead of societies and the social facts they produce. So whereas in the case of epistemological or moral scepticism, the sceptic might be said through their actions to have acknowledged an existing reality that they claim to deny, or to have exhibited a preference they claim not to have, in the case of political scepticism the society in question is actually creating the social facts in question. If these facts are brought into existence by people saying that they exist, then if enough people stop saying that they do, that is going to make a difference; certainly more of a difference than saying that a mountain doesn't exist. Social scepticism about social facts may therefore turn out to be a lot less pointless and self-defeating than other kinds of scepticism.

In that case, who or what is the sceptic? The society, or the individual? We generally think of a sceptic as an individual who doubts something, and so it is tempting to imagine that a sceptical society would consist of individuals who doubted the social facts in question. But social scepticism is different. It is not itself a representational mental state but rather an outcome of social action, and, furthermore, an outcome that is not exhaustively explained in terms of the intentions of its agents. Scepticism implies that X doubts rather than believes something, but a society's scepticism about a social fact does not necessarily imply that X, Y and Z all doubt rather than believe something, only that X, Y and Z do not all believe it, or that they do not all collectively believe it, or at least not at the same time, or in the same way, or to the same degree.

In fact, in the case of social scepticism it is not obvious that any of the individuals involved actually needs to be sceptical of anything. At least, not in the sense that they need to have considered some hypothetical social fact and then doubted it. All that would be required for social scepticism would be a form of social action that generated little or nothing in the way of social facts, and dismantled any external reasons for action that might arise. An individual sceptic might prefer to live in such a society, but that preference would not necessarily bring such a society into being even if it were widely shared. Indeed, the outcome might arise unbidden as a result of collective (in)action, without it necessarily being preferred by anyone.

On this account, social scepticism is possible not because there aren't external reasons but because there are, and because such reasons are potentially susceptible to social modification. But in that case, what sort of society would it be? Pyrrho reputedly visited India and there encountered early followers of Buddhism who, like him, considered all things to be undifferentiated, unstable and undecidable, and had left their families and withdrawn from the world. According to Megasthenes, the most honoured among these early followers of the Buddha were the forest-dwellers, 'who live in the woods on leaves and tree-fruits, wearing clothes of tree-bark, abstaining from sex and wine'.[12] That sounds suspiciously like Hume's 'life of total lethargy'. And for the individual a life of total lethargy is impossible without some loss of functionality, but what about for a society? Is there any way for a society to renounce the world without renouncing the life of the world? Nietzsche said that we must have falsehoods in order to live.[13] But maybe societies do not.

The social

Is social life possible without external reasons? Over the past two hundred years there has been growing reason to suspect that it might be. And the suggestion comes primarily from those who would rather it were not so. The thinker who addresses the issue most directly is Hannah Arendt, so let's borrow some of her terms (without any commitment to other aspects of her complex articulation of the ideas) and call the set of desire-independent reasons for action 'world'.

According to Arendt, no human life is possible without 'world'. Every human life presupposes a 'public realm', which as a 'common world, gathers us together and yet prevents our falling over each other'. That public realm is created in stages: work produces a common 'world of things', distinct from our natural surroundings, which outlasts and transcends the life of any individual.[14] Then this world of things 'is overlaid and, as it were, overgrown with an altogether different in-between, which consists of deeds and words and owes its origin exclusively to men's acting and speaking directly *to* one another'. The public realm therefore arises directly out of acting together, the 'sharing of words and deeds', and 'for all its intangibility, this in-between is no less real than the world of things we visibly have in common'.[15]

Forming a world between them saves men 'from the pitfalls of human nature'.[16] And it is 'the making and keeping of promises', which 'serves to set up in the ocean of uncertainty ... islands of security without which not even continuity, let alone durability of any kind, would be possible in the relationships between men'. Promise-making provides what Searle would call external reasons for action, and it is these that constitute a common world and our individual identities within it: 'Without being bound to the fulfilment of promises, we would never be able to keep our identities, we would wander helplessly and without direction in the darkness of each man's lonely heart'.[17]

It might appear from this that world is the inevitable product of the social relations that constitute it. But it is possible to imagine scenarios in which there is an imbalance between the two: world-heavy societies where the public realm outweighs the social relations that give rise to it, and the opposite, relatively worldless societies where the world seems inadequate to the density of the relationships that produce it. Arendt herself is preoccupied with the latter, and by the relative worldlessness of what she calls 'the social', i.e., the social relationships generated by the rise of modern mass society in which 'the world between [people] has lost its power to gather them together, to relate and to separate them'. In those circumstances

the weirdness of this situation resembles a spiritualistic séance where a number of people gathered around a table might suddenly, through some magic trick, see the table vanish from their midst.[18]

This can happen all too easily, because 'without trusting in action and speech as a mode of being together, neither the reality of one's self, of one's own identity, nor the reality of the surrounding world can be established beyond doubt'.[19] Such radical indeterminacy sounds like ancient Pyrrhonism, but Arendt claims that 'the emergence of the social realm … is a relatively new phenomenon whose origin coincided with the emergence of the modern age'. The result has been 'the eclipse of a common public world' and 'the formation of the worldless mentality'.[20]

The situation Arendt describes as 'the social' or 'society' has a sociological explanation. The common world has collapsed because 'although all men are capable of deed and word' the relentless instrumentalization of social action that characterizes the modern economy has gradually encroached upon it. One way to interpret this change might be in terms of the transition from mechanical to organic solidarity, in which a community united by common consciousness is replaced by one where people have little in common beyond the ability to coordinate their diversified social roles. And in particular Arendt's 'worldless mentality' has affinities with the abnormal form of organic solidarity that Durkheim called anomie. According to Durkheim, society normally creates rules for itself because 'social functions seek spontaneously to adapt to one another, provided they are in regular contact'. However, such rules respond to social needs that only society can feel. They emerge from 'a climate of opinion, and all opinion is a collective matter', and where that is lacking, anomie can develop. Then, any rules will be 'general and vague, for in these conditions only the most general outlines of the phenomena can be fixed'.[21]

For Durkheim and Arendt it was self-evident 'the social' and the 'anomic' were undesirable aberrations, liable to leave social life 'without cohesion and regulation', 'as floating, as futile and vain, as the wanderings of nomad tribes'.[22] But there is another way of looking at it. From the perspective of scepticism, the absence of world and of regulation are not intrinsic evils, but the natural outcome of scepticism itself. What is at issue is not the desirability of the outcome but rather its possibility, and 'the social' appears to realize the possibility of social scepticism, for it deals with social facts or rules, facts that are made and unmade by social action, but in this case unmade in such a way that there is no loss of sociability.

If its critics have described it correctly, the social would appear to answer the Humean critique of Pyrrhonism which claims that if its 'principles were universally and steadily accepted, all human life would come to an end', because in 'the social' life goes on without rules or obligations, but without any loss of functionality or complexity. The table may have disappeared, but the séance continues regardless. So maybe the social is not so much a problem as the solution to a problem. Even if there is no special way for the world to be, and the world is nevertheless always one way rather than another, there may still be some way for the world to be that better reflects the fact that there is no special way for it to be. If there is nothing that makes sense of the world, but the world keeps on making sense, then that must be because of the way that we're making it. In which case, perhaps we can remake it to make less sense than it does now, and so align it more closely with the way things are. If so, then Pyrrhonism is not just a social possibility, but a viable political project.

Making the World

How is a worldless society possible? An answer to this question requires what might appear to be a long detour, for it is difficult to respond without having an account of how the social world is made. It is only with a theory of world-making that the unmaking of the world begins to seem like a possibility. We can put the critique of scepticism to the test by turning to social ontology. Does the way the social world is made allow for the possibility that it might be unmade without loss of function? In Searle's widely influential account it does not. Despite opening the door to scepticism by accepting the existence of external reasons, he promptly closes it again by arguing that social life cannot continue without them. So, if Searle is correct, then perhaps the critics of scepticism are right after all, and there is no way to undo the world without also undoing ourselves.

According to Searle, some facts about the world are brute facts and some are social, and the former produce the latter in a seamless progression from the physical to the biological to the psychological to the social to the institutional. The world is made up of particles, such particles 'exist in fields of force, and are organized into systems'. Systems encompass everything from molecules to crystals to mountains. Some systems are living systems, and among these, some develop consciousness, and 'with consciousness comes intentionality, [which is] the capacity of the mind to represent objects and states of affairs in the world'. It is intentionality and, specifically, collective intentionality that produces social facts: 'The central span on the bridge from physics to society is collective intentionality, and the decisive movement on that bridge ... is the collective intentional imposition of function on entities that cannot perform those functions without that imposition.'[23]

How does this work? Searle provides a clearly articulated account of the construction of the social world through this route, and in the argument that follows I will be using his terminology.

Collective intention

An intentional state is a state that is *about* something, so it divides into two components: 'the type of state it is and its content, typically a propositional content' (e.g., I can believe, fear or hope that it is raining). We, like many other species of animals, have a capacity for collective intentionality which involves sharing intentional states such as beliefs and desires.[24] This happens frequently when we engage in cooperative behaviour 'where I am doing something as part of our doing something'. In such cases, rather than having different intentions, or even the same intention separately, we may have a shared intention, a 'we intention' or 'collective intention'.[25]

The difference between individual and collective intention can be seen in the following example. In one case, a group of Harvard Business School graduates, all believing in the invisible hand, go out separately, but in the knowledge that others are doing the same, to make money for themselves to the benefit of society. There is a single goal, mutual awareness that it is a shared goal, but no collective intentionality. In the other case, they all agree beforehand to do what they do in the first case. This is collective intentionality (even without further cooperation in carrying it out). The difference between the two lies not in the actions of the HBS graduates (which are the same in both cases) but in the fact that in the latter case they have an external reason because of their agreement.[26]

Social and institutional facts

The pact between the HBS graduates is a collective intentional fact, and all collective intentional facts are 'social facts'. The basic form of a social fact is 'they are doing X …' where for those involved it is a case of 'we are doing this', for example: going for a walk together, or hunting in a pack. However, there is a special subclass of social facts that are of particular importance in the making of the social world, and only those are 'institutional facts'. Unlike other social facts, an institutional fact imposes a status function. Both humans and animals have the capacity to impose functions on objects (e.g., tool use), and 'functions are always intentionality-relative'. Status functions are a special class of function performed 'not in virtue [solely] of physical structure … but in virtue of collective imposition and recognition of a status'.[27] Indeed, such a function, like the HBS pact, only exists as the result of collective acceptance or recognition. So, for example, going for a walk together is a social fact, but being part of a walking group or team is an institutional fact.

Constitutive rules

What is being accepted or recognized is a constitutive rule imposing the function in question, and 'institutional facts exist only within systems of constitutive rules'. The basic form of a constitutive rule is: 'X counts as Y in C', 'the Y-term names a power that the X-term does not have solely in virtue of its X-structure'.[28] Constitutive rules differ from regulative rules, which 'regulate antecedently existing activities'. A regulative rule like 'Drive on the Left' is satisfied by people driving on the left. But constitutive rules 'do not merely regulate, they also create the very possibility of certain activities'. For example, the rules of chess: 'the rules of chess create the very possibility of playing chess', and with that 'the possibility of abuses that could not exist without the rule'.[29]

However, constitutive rules only apply when and where they are collectively accepted. The rules of Go differ depending on whether the game is played in China or Japan, for example. And they apply only for as long as they are collectively accepted. A constitutive rule is a device for creating institutional facts by imposing status functions, but the existence of those facts consists in their 'having been created and not yet destroyed'. The continued existence of institutional facts requires that 'the individuals directly involved and a sufficient number of members of the relevant community must continue to recognise and accept the existence of such facts'. Without this, they 'will not lock into human rationality and will not provide reasons for action'.[30]

Deontic power

An institutional fact provides external reasons for action because it has deontic power. This is not some additional quality; it is merely the ability to provide reasons for acting that are independent of our inclinations, in other words 'external reasons'. According to Searle, all status functions carry deontic powers, i.e., 'rights, duties, obligations, requirements, permissions, authorizations, entitlements and so on', and 'it is because status functions carry deontic powers that they provide the glue that holds civilization together'.[31] However, all such deontic powers are conventions, and we only have external reasons for action because we have given them to ourselves. Unless the world keeps on being made in this way, it will fall apart, and a world that is falling apart isn't a social world worthy of the name. According to Searle, 'everything we value in civilization requires the creation and maintenance of institutional power relations through collectively imposed status-functions'. And if there were no deontic reasons, 'then the corresponding institutions would simply collapse'.[32]

Social ontology of the social

If this is how the social world is made, is the condition of worldlessness that Arendt describes even possible? It is clear that we cannot have a 'common world' made from the 'sharing of words and deeds' without society, but can there be society without world, or with more or less world? Searle's account appears to preclude this possibility, because, as he repeatedly states, without deontic powers (i.e., world) society would simply collapse. For Searle, institutional facts are the inevitable product of language use: 'Once you have language, it is inevitable that you will have deontology because there is no way you can make explicit speech acts performed according to the conventions of language without creating commitments.'[33] All language users have world, whereas social non-language using animals do not. To allow for the possibility of human society without a corresponding world is to undermine that distinction. There can be no complex human sociability that is not world-making, and there can be no reduction in deontic powers without a corresponding reduction in sociability.

Of course, Searle does allow for a possible loss of collective intentionality, but he assumes that, with the loss of collective intent, the corresponding institutional facts and their deontic powers punctually disappear as well: 'The moment, for example, that all or most of the members of a society refuse to acknowledge property rights … property rights cease to exist in that society.'[34] His favoured example of this is the end of Communism in Eastern Europe, which, he claims, 'collapsed when the structure of collective intentionality was no longer able to maintain the system of status functions'.[35] On this view, a world without any deontic powers, or even with weaker powers, is not so much a society free of external regulation as one that has been reduced to a lower level. In which case, the critics of scepticism are right: its principles are incompatible with a fully human life.

Although, on Searle's account, there is no space of the social, his argument nevertheless indicates clearly how and where such a space might emerge. What would have to be different for it to be possible? There would have to be fewer desire-independent reasons for acting, deontic powers that were weaker, or more thinly distributed, or maybe completely absent without any corresponding loss of social function. This would mean that the powers or functions that Searle describes were available at a lower level of social construction than the one he indicates. And this would be the case if there were, for example, institutional facts without, or with weaker, deontic powers. Everything else might be in place – the constitutive rule, even the status function declaration – but the resulting institutional fact somehow lacks power. To what extent does Searle himself allow for this possibility?

Consider two variables: the weight of the status ascribed, and the strength of the collective intention involved in making that ascription. Presumably even Searle would have to admit that some institutional facts generate a lot more power than others. For example, the status function of absolute monarch comes with a lot more deontic power than the status function of titular head of state.[36] But even if an honorary function still contains some residual deontic power, it is clear that some functions have less power than others, and that any status function can be drained of power simply by being reclassified as honorary rather than substantive. There is, in other words, a power modifier built unacknowledged into Searle's system, which, like a volume control, can be adjusted independently of the content.

But there is another dial as well: collective intention itself. Like children who only receive the wonderful presents they want if they really believe they are going to get them, we only get the institutional facts that correspond to our intention. The resulting institutional facts will have less deontic power if the collective intention that generates them is half-hearted, intermittent or patchy. A currency in which people do not have much faith, or in which not a lot of people have faith, or which they trust only now and then, will not necessarily cease to exist, but it will quickly lose its value relative to other currencies as a consequence. All of this is, of course, built into Searle's account, but he fails to make the inference that deontic power is not just present or absent but a matter of degree.[37]

If the deontic power of institutional facts can be tuned down or even out this is significant, because according to Searle the difference between an institutional fact and a merely social fact is that the former carries deontic power and the latter does not. What then is the right volume on these dials to ensure sociability? Turning them both up to the max would enhance their deontic power, but would it necessarily enhance social functionality? If so, we would have to assume that a world full of gods would at some level be more socially fit for purpose than a disenchanted world. For example, that a waning belief in the divine right of kings would necessarily make the institution of the monarchy less rather than more functional. But that is clearly not always the case. And if there's no such linear relationship, that maybe opens a space at the other end as well: perhaps, rather than being the end of civilization, a world of weak deontic powers is something that will allow us all to get on with our lives more effectively.

Rules

How might this work? Searle maintains that 'institutional facts exist only within systems of constitutive rules', but, as his critics have pointed out, social coordination appears to be possible without constitutive rules, and sometimes without rules at all. One case to which both Searle and his critics devote considerable attention serves to illustrate the limitations of his account. Suppose that there are two groups of pastoralists grazing their animals on either side of a river. The river constitutes a physical limit to their territories which they cannot cross, but when it dries up members of both groups continue to recognize it as a boundary, i.e., 'they continue to recognize that they are not supposed to cross the boundary unless authorized'. According to Searle, this 'collective recognition or acceptance by the people involved' is an example of a status function in that 'the people involved impose a status function Y on an object X in a context C'. It is 'a function that is performed by an object person or other sort of entity and which can only be performed by virtue of the fact that the community in which the function is performed assigns a certain status to the object person or entity in question, and the function is performed in virtue of that collective acceptance or rejection'.[38]

However, as Francesco Guala points out, there could be an identical outcome as the result of a correlated equilibrium in a hawk–dove game in which no constitutive rule is involved.[39] When the river dries up and the physical barrier disappears, this creates the possibility of competition and conflict between the groups. To avoid this outcome, one lot of farmers grazes by convention the land to the north and the other the land to the south. So when a farmer arrives with their cattle, they note the location and apply a conditional strategy that leads to a correlated equilibrium: '(i) Graze if the land lies north, do not graze if it lies south; (ii) Graze if the land lies south, do not graze if it lies north.' Such statements would count as regulative, not constitutive, rules in that they describe pre-existing regularities of behaviour. An external observer might conclude that the riverbed constituted the border between the two groups. A border is an institution, what Searle would term an 'institutional fact', and yet in this case no constitutive rule has been needed to establish it, or status declaration to name it, and no border exists.

If, as this implies, 'institutional terms are eliminable at no cost, constitutive rules are, at roots, just regulative rules dressed up in institutional language', then Searle's distinction breaks down, which means that his theory can be encompassed 'within a unified social ontology based on correlated equilibria and regulative rules'. For Searle, making and following a rule and having a disposition to act in a particular way are radically distinct: respecting a border is an example of an institutional fact formed from a constitutive rule, whereas having no inclination to cross a border does not even count as a social fact at all: it is more like 'animals marking the limits of their territory'.[40] But, as Guala and Hindriks argue, there is no basis for such a distinction, for 'the existence of conventions does not require an explicit formulation of the rules that ... define the correlated equilibrium'.[41] An equilibrium can be sustained simply by imitation, just as it was by the Czech and German deer who respected the Cold War border between the countries for more than one generation after the physical fence had been removed.[42]

As this example suggests, it may be impossible to distinguish an obligation from a disposition, and an obligation may be transformed into a disposition without loss of sociability.[43] Suppose the HBS graduates formed the collective intention of working in the same way for five years, and then after that period had lapsed, continued to do so, with no sense of obligation or knowledge of what others were doing, but just because that is the way they felt most comfortable working. Suppose then, that after a ten-year reunion they decided to recommit themselves to the same project for another five-year term. According to Searle, for the first and last of these periods they would have been operating according to social logic of human civilization, but in the five-year interval between these two periods they would, like animals, just have been creatures of habit and instinct. And yet, to an external observer of their working lives, nothing would have changed, and the fifteen years would appear completely seamless.

If coordination is possible without status function declarations or constitutive rules, and may emerge conventionally through rules in equilibrium, or even through disposition and habit, then there can be no important difference between institutional and social facts, or even between social facts (which require collective intention) and facts about society (which do not). Sometimes even Searle concedes as much, admitting that he does not think that there is 'a sharp dividing line between either the institutional and the non-institutional or the linguistic and the prelinguistic'.[44] And indeed, it is easy to think of examples where the transition between the two might be indiscernible. Searle often cites the fall of Communism as a case in which the lack of collective acceptance led to the disappearance of the institutional facts, discounting the possibility that the population may have lacked the collective intentions needed to sustain the institutional facts of Communism for some time, while still successfully living out the daily reality of state socialism. If worldly and worldless social states can be functionally equivalent, the social is possible.

Grounds and frames

Searle's problem, as Brian Epstein points out, is that he does not distinguish adequately between the grounding conditions of a social fact and the principles that frame it. A grounding condition is what has to be the case for a fact to obtain. A frame principle, on the other hand, is what specifies the grounding conditions for a state of affairs (i.e., social fact) in a possible world. Frame principles provide the basis for ascription, rather than being performatives themselves; they do not invest with power; they merely indicate what the grounding conditions are. In some cases, those grounding conditions might involve collective intention (what counts as a dollar bill), in others not (what counts as a mob).[45]

If we identify a number of people running down the street as a mob, it is not as a result of some collective intention or convention they are following in their behaviour, but our conventions (linguistic/legal/political) about the identification of mobs. Epstein's point is that we don't need communal agreement to make X into Y (e.g., a number of people running into a mob), only to know when it is that X counts as Y (e.g., what constitutes a mob). And in such cases, what anchors the frame may be quite different from what grounds the social fact, and there is scope for pluralism in both cases.[46] So, although some social facts may be grounded in collective intention and status function declaration, there is no need to assume that all are, and the fact that collective acceptance of a frame principle may be required is not indication that the social fact in question is itself grounded in collective intention.

There can be facts about society that are not social facts as Searle describes them because they do not involve collective intention, and rather than being made they are simply observed and described. There is therefore a significant difference between making the world and acting in the world in such a way that it fits a particular frame. Searle actually acknowledges this possibility at the macroscopic level. He does not claim that society as a whole is an institutional fact or even a social fact: '"society" does not name a form of collective intentionality ... [because] it is only a social fact if there is a collective intentionality shared by the members of the society'. According to him, things like society are better described as 'systemic fallouts or consequences of ground-floor institutional facts' or 'third person fallout facts from institutional facts', third person 'because they need not be known by participants in the institution ... [but] can be stated from a third-person anthropological point of view. They carry no additional deontology'.[47]

However, if this applies to society as a whole, there seems no reason why it should not also apply to its constituent parts. If society as a whole is a fallout fact rather than an institutional fact, then why should not at least some of the facts that ground it be fallout facts as well, the unintended consequences of social action rather than the result of collective intentionality. This may well be the case in many of the examples cited. It is the third-person observer who identifies the property of the two groups of pastoralists and the border between the Czech and German deer on the basis of a frame principle unknown to the participants and anchored in the observer's experience and not in theirs. These are fallout facts without any ground-floor institutional facts at all, and fallout facts do not make the world, they only describe it.

The original question was 'Is scepticism possible?' Searle's defence of external reasons provides (against the Humean critique) a basis for thinking that it might be. But only if, contrary to what Searle himself claims, those external reasons (in the form of deontic powers) can be weakened or forgotten without corresponding loss of sociability. So, the first question leads to a second: Is a worldless, or at the least, less worldly sociability possible for humans, just as it is for animals and might be for robots? Can social life go on, without any loss of functionality or complexity, sustained by instinct, habit and spontaneous adaption but with fewer rules or obligations or declarations? The critical account of Searle's social ontology given here suggests that it can, and that society can be divested of world in ways that Arendt and Durkheim indicate might be possible, but that Searle himself does not allow.[48] So, maybe scepticism is possible after all, if not for individuals then for societies. In which case, perhaps one of the potential functions of society is to help rid us of the illusions to which we might otherwise be enslaved.

Unmaking the World

The problem is this: even if there is no particular way the world ought to be, society will keep on making the world regardless, and the world that results will be one way rather than another. This might seem to imply that the sceptical project is doomed because the actions of sceptics will continue to construct the world to which they would deny plausibility, and there is no way society could ever be in which scepticism about society could be realized. But that's not necessarily the case, because there do seem to be societies that are relatively worldless and anomic. Perhaps such societies suggest an answer to the problem of how society might realize the possibility of scepticism.

Using Searle's account of social construction it became clear that there are ways in which we might make less world (and make less of the world) and that there might be a distinct social ontology of the social, i.e., a way of rebuilding the world as we go along so that it amounts to less. What would this be like? Think of Otto Neurath's boat:

> We are like sailors who on the open sea must reconstruct their ship
> but are never able to start afresh from the bottom. Where a beam is
> taken away a new one must at once be put there, and for this the rest
> of the ship is used as support. In this way, by using the old beams
> and driftwood the ship can be shaped entirely anew, but only by
> gradual reconstruction.[49]

In this scenario, when one plank is removed another is
substituted, and so although by the end nothing remains
of the original, the ship has been remade without loss. But
the sceptical crew soon realizes that much of this labour is
superfluous; the process of rebuilding itself shows that none
of the original planks was essential and that it is possible to
stay afloat with less than the full inventory of operational
parts. As the voyage progresses, the ship will continually
be redesigned so that it has fewer planks yet still remains
seaworthy. And, in the end, if there aren't enough planks
to make a hull, the sailors can always plane them into surf-
boards, and learn how to surf.

Deontological parsimony

What sort of replacements are involved in this transformation and what sort of loss? It is apparent that even within
Searle's social ontology there are various routes through
which this might come about, whether through the weakening of collective intentions, constitutive rules or social
conventions. But is there a principle that underlies them all,
a single blueprint for the deconstruction of Neurath's boat?
Their common feature is deontological parsimony, i.e.,
they all minimise deontic power. This is a novel concept

and so it is important to differentiate it from related ideas like epistemological restraint on the one hand and ontological parsimony on the other.

Deontological parsimony refers not to what is knowable but to what there is, in this case institutional facts with deontic powers. It therefore differs from epistemological restraint or abstinence, ideas that are to be found in the debates around Rawls's theory of justice, and merely imply impartiality between different truth claims and a version of the good life rather than scepticism about them.[50] However, although he denied it, Rawls's assumption that 'there is no conception of the good that nobody could reasonably reject', would appear to presuppose some degree of underlying scepticism: not necessarily a strong claim that all belief is ill-founded, but a moderate scepticism to the effect that, when it comes to the social and political good, all certainty is ill-founded.[51] And it is precisely the view that underlies deontological parsimony as well. Here, we are not talking about an epistemological scepticism applied to politics but a socially mediated scepticism in which the scepticism is to be found not in the premiss but in the outcome. Deontological parsimony is not about explanation, it's about how many obligations we create for ourselves, how many rods we fashion for our own backs.

In this respect, deontological parsimony has more in common with what Quine called ontological parsimony: the idea that entities are not to be multiplied beyond necessity, and that, other things being equal, a theory that is more ontologically parsimonious is to be preferred to one that is less so.[52] But in the case of social scepticism what is required is not ontological parsimony but deontological. The concept of the social describes a form of society in which there is a low ratio of deontological to ontological commitments. If such a society is possible, then it must allow for the possibility that deontology is distinct from ontology and that an ontological jungle might become a deontological desert (and vice versa).

Searle thinks that ontological and deontological commitments are made in the same way and often at the same time: 'Once we have an explicit language in which explicit speech acts can be performed according to the conventions of language we already have a deontology ... because there is no way you can make explicit speech acts performed according to the conventions of language without creating commitments.'[53] But even on Searle's terms, it is possible to construct a social ontology in which there is a low ratio of institutional facts to social facts, whether by taking away the deontic power of existing social facts, or by creating more social facts without deontic powers. What would the mechanisms for this be? In social scepticism, it is society itself that acts as Occam's razor as we find ways to relate to each other that are less deontologically prodigal. Deontological parsimony means less collective intention, and that means transforming collective intentions into an aggregation of individual intentions, and/or intentional into non-intentional states.

What sort of razor is it? Elliott Sober makes a useful distinction between the razor of silence and the razor of denial: 'The first says that you should *not believe* hypotheses that aren't needed to explain; the second says that you should *disbelieve* such hypotheses.'[54] The problem with the razor of denial is that it presents itself as an exception to its own rule, and so is liable to invest itself with the very powers that it drains from other hypotheses. As Bruno Latour argues, using the razor of denial too freely to desacralize the idols of the tribe both confirms their power and fetishizes the act of desecration, so rather than eliminating the fetish character of the world it multiplies it: the anti-fetish becomes a fetish itself, or a 'factish' as Latour calls it.[55]

It was a problem that already engaged the ancient scep-tics, among whom it was recognized that being too dogmatic might make scepticism less consistent and also less plausible. Pyrrho's own mode of life illustrates the razor of silence, and Timon affirms that 'the outcome for those who actually adopt this attitude … will be first *aphasia* speechlessness'.[56] Suspension of judgement meant affirming neither one thing nor its contrary, in other words not affirming anything at all. So, scepticism does not use the razor of denial, but if it is social it cannot always be a razor of literal silence. How would this work? According to Sextus Empiricus, what sceptics are doing when they speak is not affirming 'that things certainly are just as we say they are'; they are, rather, reporting on how things appear at the time 'with-out any belief, affirming nothing about external objects'.[57] So someone might just resign themselves to the impression they were left with, without coming to any judgement as to whether it was true. That is not necessarily incapacitat-ing. One does not need to believe in order to act, and the sceptic may behave 'exactly in the way in which somebody who believed these views to be true would behave'.[58] In such cases, there is no collective mind-to-world fit, no 'we intend', indeed no intentionality at all, just a neutral report on the contents of an individual consciousness.

Searle allows for this possibility, sometimes using the hybrid notion of 'collective recognition or acceptance' to mark 'a continuum from enthusiastic endorsement to just going along with the structure'. As Searle concedes, collective recognition 'is a much weaker form' of collective attitude than collective intention, but he does not draw the implication that the deontic powers associated with it will be weaker as a result.[59] It is not clear that collective recognition alone will give rise to constitutive rules, and institutions that depend on it will be different to those that have full deontic powers. And there obviously comes a point at which recognition shades into observation, and all we are left with are fallout facts that do not qualify social facts at all.

Furthermore, 'going along with' may not always involve a separate moment of assent or acquiescence. Arcesilaus was the first to point out that the impression, assent, impulse sequence can easily be contracted to omit assent.[60] And as Michael Frede comments, the impulse that follows an impression 'may be all acquiescence and assent consist in'. Perhaps it is wrong to assume that we are constantly judging things to be one way or another and 'that action ordinarily involves assent (e.g., in walking down the street, assenting to the impression that this is a street, this is a man, etc., in such a way as to walk down the street, not bump into the man, etc.)'.[61] In such cases we are just taking things for granted, using our experience to negotiate our environment without making any judgement about it all or having any intentional stance towards it. Perhaps the sceptic can be active, yet still not be 'acting in the robust sense of the dogmatist's theory of human action'.[62] If such a way of proceeding permits sociability, then it is a deontologically parsimonious form of social action in which society is functioning without deontic powers, or at least with relatively few with respect to those generated through collective intention.

Deontic power has a specific meaning within Searle's ontology: it is where 'the Y-term names a power that the X term does not have solely in virtue of its X-structure'.[63] Deontological parsimony can therefore operate in several ways: (i) Where the content of the Y-term is modified so that the Y-term more closely resembles the X-structure, then what will be in question is not whether the deontic power exists or not at any given moment, but rather the extent of its power. In contrast, (ii) where there is weak collective intention, or only collective recognition instead of cooperation, then it is the naming of the Y-term that is threatened, for the weaker the intention the less certainty there is that the Y-term has actually been named, or recognized, or that the level of recognition has been such that it has reached a threshold to be designated at all. Weak content is deinstitutionalizing, and is liable to reduce institutional to social facts, and social facts to brute facts which have no deontic powers at all. Alternatively, (iii) where the moment of assent is absent altogether, i.e., where constitutive rules give way to a regulative equilibrium, then there is no naming and no Y-term either, and the deontic power disappears altogether even when the practice it regulated continues in a way that is functionally equivalent and capable of being identified as such by a competent observer.

These forms of deontological parsimony are neither exhaustive nor mutually exclusive, and the extent to which the outcome is deontologically as opposed to ontologically parsimonious will vary accordingly. Take a simple fetish object to which sacred powers are attributed. If (i) the content of the beliefs about it is weakened it becomes a weak fetish; if (ii) belief itself is weakened it becomes a fetish whose powers are intermittent and unpredictable. If (iii) collective intention gives way to regulative equilibrium, it may be secularized so that although formally recognized no one is sure whether anyone believes in it or not. And if the conventions (grounds or frames) that sustain it are weakened then its sacred powers may become increasingly fuzzy: Do they inhere in the object or its location or the rituals, etc.? In practice, of course, all of these things may happen at the same time and to varying degrees. With property rights deontological parsimony might mean (i) weak property rights, (ii) rights weakly held or attributed, or (iii) as Guala suggests might happen in the case of regulative equilibrium, 'the theoretical term property can in principle be dispensed with, by formulating the theory entirely in regulative language'.[64]

What about something more complex like money? As Searle notes, money is the product of fantasy: 'As long as everyone shares the fantasy and has confidence in it, the system will work just fine. But when some of the fantasies cease to be believable … then the whole system begins to unravel.'[65] But what does ceasing to be believable mean?

What forms might unravelling take? Money can be abolished, at great social cost (which is ontologically reductive). The currency can be changed (which is ontologically transformative, but deontologically constant); more often, however, a currency fluctuates in value, with lack of belief resulting in inflation (a nice example of deontological parsimony combined with ontological prodigality), or is reduced to regulative rules or conventions with a loss of exclusivity as legal tender as it is undermined by black market currencies or barter.

The razor that effects deontological parsimony is a razor of the collectively unsaid (no constitutive rules/status declarations) and the collectively understated (withdrawal of extent, intensity or content of collective acceptance), a razor of collective inattention and collective forgetfulness. But insofar as it is social, it is not a matter of individual intentions, or the lack of them, but rather of the way individual intentions or their lack can converge and combine. Using that razor we can potentially cut back deontic powers until they disappear entirely, but there are as many ways to do so as there are degrees of parsimony and types of institutional fact.

Dereification

What might deontological parsimony look like as a social project, and where would it lead? What the examples above have in common is that they all break with the illusory objectivity of institutional facts and recover their contingency. And there is already a name for that: dereification.[66] In his essay of 1922, 'Reification and the Consciousness of the Proletariat', Georg Lukács argued that reification is necessarily the experience of everyone living in a capitalist society because the essence of the commodity-structure is that 'a relation between people takes on the character of a thing and thus acquires a "phantom objectivity"'. People lose sight of the contingency of social facts and forget that they are social, i.e., formed by the relations between people, and as a result they become crystallized into 'an ossified, impenetrable thing alienated from man'.[67]

It is an argument that can readily be translated into the language of social ontology. As Michael J. Thompson observes, 'the concept of reification can be reconstructed along the lines of a form of collective-intentional set of constitutive rules that assign statuses and functions to social relations, social roles, social practices, and so on, that in turn grant domination relations and other forms of power their legitimacy, resilience, social acceptance and legitimacy.' Social facts become alien through being invested with deontic powers and becoming external reasons for action. In this context deontological parsimony emerges as a form of 'non-reified thought (i.e., critical reasoning)', which is what comes into play 'whenever we see that any social fact is in fact not a distinct thing, object or entity in and of itself', but is rather constituted by social relationships.[68]

Marx had famously likened the commodity to the fetish, because in the commodity 'the social character of men's labour appears to them as an objective character stamped upon the product of that labour' in a way that has 'absolutely no connection with their physical properties and with the material relations arising therefrom'.[69] The objects of labour become alien through becoming private property. However, as Lukács argues, this process of alienation can be reversed precisely because it is a form of social ontology in which the proletariat is not just the object but also the subject of the process, and so can become aware of itself as such, and act accordingly:

> The specific nature of this kind of commodity had consisted in the fact that beneath the cloak of the thing lay a relation between men, that beneath the quantifying crust, there was a qualitative, living core. Now that this core is revealed it becomes possible to recognise the fetish character *of every commodity* based on the commodity character of labour power: in every case we find its core, the relation between men, entering into the evolution of society.[70]

But although grounded in a transformed self-consciousness, reification can only be overcome through practice, in other words, though the practical abolition of institutional facts 'as the *actual forms of social life*'. For only when 'the theoretical primacy of the "facts" has been broken, only when *every phenomenon is recognised to be a process*, will it be understood that what we are wont to call "facts" consists of processes.'[71]

In this context, the transition from exchange value to use value, the withering away of the state when its class basis is superseded, and the demystification of ideology are all forms of deontological parsimony. Indeed, as Bertell Ollman observes, every fixed social category (i.e., every institutional fact) must be dissolved, because 'erasing social lines *per se* ... is a major task of the dictatorship of the proletariat'.[72] The result, according to Marx, is the end of 'human self-estrangement … the complete restoration of man to himself as a *social* ie. human being … the genuine resolution of the conflict between man and nature'.[73] De-reification means that man returns to the experience, though not the condition, of 'the savage in his cave … [who] does not experience his environment as alien; [but] feels just as much at home as a fish in water', and ceases to be 'a stranger in the world that he himself has made'.[74]

If praxis, i.e., social action that unmakes the world, turns out to be the best response to the apraxia challenge, then it may not be entirely fortuitous. Like Hegel before him, Lukács was influenced by scepticism.[75] And while Hegel dismissed modern scepticism as an 'excuse for nonphilosophy', he also valued ancient Pyrrhonism for its dismissal of common-sense thinking about the material world and for its adumbration of the dialectic in equipollence, the juxtaposition of contradictory ideas equally likely to be true. According to Marcuse in *Reason and Revolution*, Hegel's account of scepticism shows that man can know the truth only if he breaks through his reified world, 'an alienated estranged world, in which man does not recognize or fulfil himself', and feeds directly into Marx's theory of dealienation. Marcuse is here reading both Hegel and Marx through the optic of Lukács, but in the process he allows us to glimpse something significant: the affinity between scepticism and praxis, and the potential for social praxis to make us feel at home in the world in ways that individual scepticism cannot.[76]

The Background

So, what would a dereified world actually be like, and to what extent would it converge with the worldless world of Arendt's imaginary? Searle gives a description of a deontologically inert environment in his account of what he calls the 'Background'. The concept emerges from his realization that 'intentional states do not function autonomously' because 'it is always possible to offer alternative interpretations of any intentional content'. There would be, for example, no way of telling how the practice of 'cutting a cake' might differ from 'cutting the grass' unless you had some familiarity with both activities. Searle calls all this assorted know-how the Background. It is 'not a set of things nor a set of mysterious relations between ourselves and things, rather it is simply a set of skills, stances, pre-intentional assumptions and presuppositions, practices, and habits'.[77] It is a 'knowing how' rather than a 'knowing that', but it is a 'knowing how' that enables us to 'know that'. It is what is presupposed by the social world of collective intention, while remaining distinct from it: 'a set of nonrepresentational mental capacities that enable all representing to take place'.[78]

Precisely because the social world relies on the Background, it can also be collapsed into it. Searle argues that 'some, though not all, the intentionalistic apparatus can be explained in terms of, and ultimately eliminated in favour of the "Background" of capacities, abilities, tendencies, and dispositions.' This can happen because of the 'parallelism between the functional structure of the Background and the intentional structure of the social phenomena to which the Background capacities relate'. It is often the case that 'we just know what to do, we just know how to deal with the situation. We do not apply the rules consciously or unconsciously.' And as we learn how to do things 'we evolve a set of dispositions that are sensitive to the rule structure'. The rules are then gradually dispensed with, so that by the end none of the original instructions has any relevance.[79]

Searle himself provides a description:

> Consider what it is like to learn how to ski. The beginning skier is given a set of verbal instructions as to what he is supposed to do: 'lean forward', 'bend the ankles', 'keep the weight on the down-hill ski' ... As the skier gets better he does not internalize the rules better, but rather the rules become progressively irrelevant ... [until] the repeated practice enables the body to take over and the rules to recede into the Background.[80]

This process is not the kind of thing we usually have in mind when we think about scepticism. But it is a perfect example, the short-circuiting of Arcesilaus's impression-assent-impulse sequence to exclude assent. At one point the skier might have asked themselves, 'What am I meant to do now?' and replied 'Lean forward', and then leant forward. But with practice they discover the truth of the claim that it is a dogmatic fantasy that action always involves assent. And in the process, it becomes apparent that scepticism itself, i.e., non-assent, may be not a negation but an omission, and an unconscious one at that, the result not of thought but of practice.

Acting without believing may be compatible with individual epistemological scepticism, but it will count as social scepticism only in the case of social action without collective intention, for deontological parsimony is the outcome of social not individual (in)action. Another of Searle's examples can be adapted (from baseball to basketball, and from the individual to the team) in order to illustrate the point:

> Suppose a group of kids learns how to play basketball. At the beginning they actually learn a set of rules, principles, and strategies. But after they get skilled, their behaviour becomes much more fluent, much more melodic, much more responsive to the demands of the situation. In such a case ... they are not applying the rules more skilfully; rather, they have acquired a set of dispositions or skills to respond appropriately.[81]

If a basketball team collectively absorbs the rules and techniques of basketball to the extent that for everyone involved they become a set of internalized dispositions and skills, then it will also be on this basis that the players communicate with each other. There is nothing unusual about this: according to Searle 'it is a precondition of our attempting to communicate that we take other organisms like ourselves as sharing the same background capacities'.[82] But it is significant nevertheless, for it means that basketball becomes a form of sociability coordinated and communicated without deontic powers. The table has been taken away, but the séance continues.

Basketball operates within a very 'local', culturally specific Background, but there must also be a 'deep' Background of natural instincts and species-wide skills and social traits which underlies other layers of more local backgrounds of habits, skills and practices. As Searle acknowledges, 'without some degree of shared Background, it is hard to see how a society could function'. And so 'though "society" does not name a form of collective intentionality, there are Background practices, presuppositions, and so on that are typically shared by the members of a society'.[83] In other words, the Background provides the grounding for something that might be recognized within the appropriate frame as society, but that something is also nothing, because it is not made through collective intention and is not itself an institutional fact, and therefore not part of a social world at all within Searle's own terms. Searle himself thinks of society as a 'fallout fact' from all the institutional facts that make up the social world. But if what unites the members of a society is a shared Background, then no institutional facts may be necessary for that fallout fact to be recognized as such, and society as a whole could be said to be a latent function of the Background without a 'social world'.

Having derived the social world from the natural, for Searle, the world unmade is by default the natural world. The farmers who observe their invisible boundary may be like animals marking their territory, but this is not a regression to nature so much as a naturalization of a socially complex world, and a dissolution of the boundary between the social and the natural. The Background is neither wholly physiological nor intentional, and, as Searle acknowledges, it has something in common with Foucault's bio-power.[84] It means that someone 'has developed a set of capacities and abilities that render him at home in that society; and … the man at home in his society is as comfortable as the fish in the sea or the eyeball in its socket'.[85]

According to Arendt, this is precisely what happens in the social where 'none of the higher capacities of man was any longer necessary to connect individual life with the life of the species; [and] individual life became part of the life process'. A 'socialized mankind' such as Marx had in mind 'consists of worldless specimens of the species mankind', because all that is left is natural force, 'the force of the life process itself, to which all men and all human activities were equally submitted'. When that happens labour itself 'is oblivious to the world to the point of worldlessness' and every human activity takes on the character of a natural phenomenon, just as in Marx's famous example of dealienated labour in which Milton is said to have 'produced *Paradise Lost* in the way that a silkworm produces silk, as the expression of *his own* nature'.[86]

However, even if the social is part of the Background, not all of the Background is the social, for much of the Background is just nature. The intensity and complexity of social interaction differs both between and within species. There is Milton and there are silkworms, and both are naturally productive, but there is a discernible difference in the complexity of what they produce and the way they produce it. The social is therefore that part of the Background that is like the rest of nature in being deontologically inert, but unlike other parts of nature in its level of social complexity. Complex social interaction is facilitated by deontic powers and for that reason it is often deontologically prodigal. But if deontologically parsimonious forms of complex sociability are possible, then the social becomes a second, socially constructed, nature, the result not of total lethargy, but of a specifically deontological inertia.

Nietzsche claimed that Pyrrho sought only 'to live a lowly life among the lowly ... To live in the common way, to honor and believe what all believe.'[87] That is not a bad description of what fading into the Background might be like. The Pyrrhonist approach was to go along with the way things appeared to be (in other words, the way most people took them to be) without affirming that they were so. In other words, operating within the functional structure of the social world without contributing to the intentional one that forms it. In this way, it was possible to develop the set of skills necessary to negotiate the social world without endorsing any particular beliefs about it. It is all about fitting into the world as you find it, without making any judgement about it, perhaps without even noticing that it is there. And that doesn't have to be as dull as Nietzsche makes it sound. Think of Neurath's sailors surfing on the open ocean.

Scepticism and Power

If scepticism is warranted, and 'the social' is possible, then although scepticism may not provide an argument for the social, it nevertheless leads us to interact in ways in which society becomes less worldly than it was before. Sceptics are not obliged to act this way, and they need not even share the intention to make the world less worldly. It is just that deontologically parsimonious social action is the only form of social action compatible with scepticism, and that the social is the (perhaps unintended) consequence.

It is therefore wrong to claim that scepticism has no consequences for politics, for the realization that social scepticism will result in a particular type of society opens up the possibility not merely of a political scepticism (i.e., a healthy scepticism about politics) but a politics of scepticism. What form should we expect this to take? Pyrrhonism is said to have emerged as a protest against political power. According to Diogenes Laertius, Pyrrho, who had himself received a large sum for a poem in praise of Alexander, was prompted to adopt his new way of life and thought by an Indian philosopher who had criticized Pyrrho's teacher Anaxarchus for paying court to kings.[88] If that is true, scepticism developed as a form of resistance to the alliance of power and knowledge.

If scepticism in politics is collectively realizable in ways that individual scepticism about epistemology and ethics is not, what are the consequences? According to the ancient sceptics, 'we are brought first to *epoche* and then to *ataraxia*'.[89] *Epoche* is a suspension of judgement based on the balance between opposing but equal arguments, and it produces *ataraxia*: tranquillity, or the absence of worry. Translated into the terms of social ontology: we are free of disturbance because there are no deontic powers over us. From this perspective, scepticism is about freedom from external power. But whereas Pyrrhonism held out the illusory promise of complete personal freedom from the external world, social scepticism is about collective rather than personal emancipation. And what are we liberated from? The world that we have made, and cannot entirely help ourselves from making, and the strange power that it exercises over us, its makers.

How does this happen? If, as Searle claims, the core notion of power is that 'A has power over S with respect to action B if and only if A can intentionally get S to do what A wants regarding B, whether S wants to do it or not', and 'power between human beings is normally exercised through the performance of speech acts', then it follows that 'all political power is deontic power'.[90] A deontologically parsimonious society is therefore one in which we collectively free ourselves from political power along with other forms of deontology. But how could we ever manage to do that when deontic powers enable us to do so many things we would not otherwise be able to do? The possibility of freedom exists because, in 'the social', deontic powers aren't necessarily a prerequisite for sociability. What 'the social' demonstrates is that complex sociability can take place without the aid of status functions or deontic powers, and that rather than living in the world we can live at least partially in the Background instead, without any loss of functionality.

Scepticism implies that we don't know who should have power over whom, but some do nevertheless have power over others, and social agency plays a significant role in determining who they are. If scepticism destroys anything it is therefore the idea of legitimate power. But scepticism does not necessarily make power disappear altogether; it may just change its form and its degree of potency. Deontic power may be reduced to instrumental power or brute power (or some combination of the two). The effect is, in the former case, to turn a status function into an agentive function with instrumental power, and in the latter to reduce deontic to brute power. As an example of the first, we might think of the difference between a postman and a messenger. The former has a uniform and a set of rights and duties that includes the delivery of messages to their recipients. The messenger does the same thing with no rights or duties, though being a messenger necessarily requires a certain level of involvement and competence in the delivery of messages. As an example of the second: consider the difference between a monarch and a person standing on the top of a hill who is well placed to push others down again. The latter may call themselves 'king of the hill', but we all know that's just brute power talking; yet in the case of the King or Queen of England it's far less clear. Social scepticism potentially reduces postmen to messengers and kingdoms to hills. It is worth considering both possibilities in more detail.

Instrumentalizing power

According to Åsa Andersson, who has developed Searle's social ontology of power, there are two types of normative social power: deontic and instrumental (or, as she prefers to call it, 'telic'). Deontic power cannot exist without the existence of institutions, while instrumental powers can, because a social practice is sufficient for this type of power to exist. Consider the example of the knife: 'Given the *purpose* of a knife to cut things ... the ideal knife is extremely sharp and cuts through almost everything.'[91] Instrumental powers are the things a person or an object has to have or do in order to perform a particular function. Instrumental power in this sense comes with what Searle calls agentive function, the function imposed on an object used for a certain purpose: 'whenever the function of x is to y then x is *supposed* to cause or otherwise result in y' even if it doesn't (e.g., the function of safety valves is to prevent explosions even if they don't).[92]

It is not only objects that have agentive functions. For example, certain individuals in our society are accredited as medical doctors because they are believed to be equipped to cure people's ailments, but there are also people who practise medicine in the sense that they cure people's ailments. There may be considerable overlap between the two groups, yet the grounds for membership will be different: in the former case it is a deontic power, in the latter it is a causal or instrumental power. Social scepticism withdraws that accreditation, with the consequence that there are no more medical practitioners with the right to practise medicine. But although there may be no more licensed medical practitioners, there will still be those who have the related agentive function.[93]

Social scepticism transforms deontic into instrumental power. With deontic power, 'X counts as Y in C', and 'the Y-term names a power that the X-term does not have solely in virtue of its X-structure'. However, without the collective intention that X should count as Y in C, X does not count as Y, so either the Y disappears and we are left with X counts as X in C, or the power that Y names is reduced to a power that it does have in virtue of its X-structure. In both cases Ys disappear from our world, but Xs do not. And so messengers can go on delivering letters without being postmen. And cardboard boxes can go on functioning as seats even when they stop being thrones, because establishing whether a cardboard box will serve as a chair (as opposed to a throne) is something that can be achieved by sitting on it.

The ease with which deontic can be transformed into instrumental power reflects the ease with which it happens the other way around. It is a small but unnecessary step from the recognition of an agentive function to the creation of a related deontic power. And because it is so simple for instrumental powers to be transformed into deontic ones, deontological parsimony must involve not only transforming deontic to instrumental powers but also impeding the transformation of instrumental into deontic powers. One way to do this is through not just deinstitutionalizing but also deintentionalizing action. This means transforming intentional action into unconscious habit, and agentive into nonagentive function, i.e., a function that does not fulfil a human intention (though it may be a latent function that is a result of human intention, but not the intended function).

Not only is it possible to exercise a social skill without the deontic power to do so, but also without the intention of doing so. On this account, there are potentially two different phases to scepticism in social ontology: the first involves the move from constitutive to regulative rules, and status to agentive functions; the second from regulative rule to inclination, and agentive to non-agentive (or latent) function. In which case, the instrumentalization of deontic power is a step towards the habitualization of social action that allows rules of any type to recede into the Background. The latter move might seem unnecessary in terms of deontological parsimony, but it prevents instrumental power from being transmuted into deontic power through the collective intentionality required to sustain an agentive function becoming the basis for the imposition of a status function.

Consider another of Searle's sporting examples.[94] Suppose a coach comes across a group of kids playing a game according to the regulative rules of baseball, without knowing that it is baseball. They can be told: this is baseball, and if you agree to make your existing regulative rules constitutive rules, you can join the Baseball Association. But if all those manoeuvres have become unconscious habits, which they engage in without knowing that they are playing baseball, perhaps without any awareness that they are playing a game, or even perhaps that they are playing, then there is no such easy transposition, because it is much more difficult to transform a latent function into a status function than it is an agentive function. As Epstein points out, you can recognize a mob quite easily, but coming up with the rules to form one is much more difficult. And the same is true of baseball, if it's being played without rules.

Brutalizing power

The other alternative to deontic power is brute power. Brute power is the product not just of physical strength, but of skill, speed and intelligence. It is power that owes more to our natural advantages as individuals than to social agreement, and as power-over it is synonymous with power exercised through violence and without consent. However, brute force also needs deontic power to survive. Although pure brute force does exist, it is the prerogative of the robber and the extortionist and extremely limited in scope (in both time and space). No individual or criminal gang can sustain a monopoly of violence across a wide expanse of time and space through intimidation alone, because there are always liable to be places or times when they lack superior strength.

More extensive and sustained violence requires some form of social organization or chain of command. The forms of violence that carry political weight all acquire and maintain their power through social organization and the deontic powers ascribed to individuals and units alike. Deontic power is needed to smooth over the gaps in time and space; to establish power without the need to enforce it at every moment. For this reason, violence is also one of the most deontologically creative of human activities. There is little point to brute force unless it can be translated into deontic power. Indeed, brute power might be said to aspire to the condition of deontic power, because deontic powers may be total. Brute power therefore inclines to deontological prodigality in a way that instrumental power is not, because whereas instrumental power has its own ends, the end of brute power is deonticity.

It is possible to imagine how deontic power might be reduced to brute power, for very often deontic powers rely on, and serve to disguise, brute force in the first place. In political theory, social order may emerge from the freely given consent of individuals in the state of nature, but in political history, it usually derives from the acquiescence of the defeated.[95] Scepticism calls into question the deontic force of victors everywhere, and stripped of those powers brute force may be all that is left. The collective realization that their divinely appointed kings, rightful lords, natural rulers, etc. are in fact no more than other people with more lethal weapons has been the first step towards liberation for many subject peoples and groups. However, it is more complicated than that, for brute force and deontic power are often inextricably interwoven with the result that violence is as much the servant of deontic power as the other way around, and often both simultaneously. While collective acceptance is enough for most forms of deontic power, political power requires both collective acceptance and the threat of violence. As Searle observes, the paradox of government is that political power is 'a system of status functions and thus rests on collective acceptance, but the collective acceptance, though not itself based on violence, can continue to function only if there is a permanent threat of violence'.[96]

Reducing deontic power to brute power is not straightforward, for if government is a form of deontic power that requires the threat of violence, deontic and prudential reasons for action are inextricably fused, and it is impossible to attenuate one without simultaneously attenuating the other. Weakening deontic power undermines a government's claim to obedience, which weakens the effectiveness of its armoury, because the more state violence approximates to common crime, the less willing its agents are to commit it. Undermining brute power makes the deontic claims of the powerful less plausible. So deontological parsimony will not only reduce deontic to brute power; it will, where they are conjoined, reduce the two together.

Scepticism cannot make brute force disappear any more than it can make the external world disappear, but in reducing deontic to brute power social scepticism not only brutalizes power but attenuates it: where brute power is the servant of deontic power, social scepticism delegitimates it and makes it unusable; where deontic power creates a chain of command, social scepticism frustrates the articulation and exercise of brute power; and where deontic power provides the motive for violence, social scepticism renders it meaningless. And since deontological parsimony also involves preventing new deontic powers from coming into being, and the object of war is to obtain deontic power over others by brute force, deontological parsimony entails either the reduction of war to mindless violence or the elimination of war itself. For if there are no deontic powers, there is no reason to go to war save for a delight in destruction for its own sake.

Equipotency

Deontological parsimony affects not only the quantity of brute power but also its distribution. Without the benefit of deontic powers to articulate and extend it, the brute force that any one individual can muster will be radically diminished and not all that different from anyone else's. Considering the huge discrepancies in the power wielded by different people, it soon becomes clear that the differential is a result of their respective deontic powers and that their brute strength is far more equally matched, just as it would be between two animals of any other species. Differentials do exist as the result of a combination of genetic and environmental factors, but it is possible to see how massively these are amplified through deontic power. Historically, human males have often been somewhat larger and stronger than females, but that small differential has been the basis of multiple forms of patriarchy (i.e., deontic powers formed for the benefit of men), in many of which women have been reduced to little more than slaves.

Brutalizing power is therefore paradoxically one way of equalizing power. And equalizing power is one way to ensure that power stays brutal. It will be more deontologically parsimonious to have a distribution of brute power in which deontic claims do not gain traction (because they can never be upheld by a preponderance of brute force) than one in which they are forever being formulated and rejected. Unequal distributions of brute power are to be avoided because the most deontologically parsimonious equilibrium is equipotency, and deontological inertia is only sustainable in an ontology that does not foster deontic claims. The reduction of brute power to equipotency is not only a consequence of the reduction of deontic power, but its prerequisite, and thus a direct objective of deontological parsimony in its own right.

For any collectivity this translates into a balance of power between its various parts; i.e., it means that no brute power is better able to create deontic power than any other. For example, the Background is deontologically inert, so it can have no space for deontic powers, but can it allow differentials in brute power? Searle never addresses the issue, yet it is difficult to see how it could, because in the case of the Background, 'provided that there is indeed a set of shared Background norms, *anybody* can exercise power over *anybody* else'. In other words, 'anybody who accepts the

Background presuppositions and knows that these presuppositions are widely shared in the community can exercise power over anybody who violates these presuppositions', but at the same time they are 'also a subject of power', because anybody can impose the same sanctions against them.[97] So everyone is equally and interchangeably able to exercise power over everyone else, in a way that would not be the case with significant differentials in brute power, because otherwise the weak would be afraid of exercising their Background power over the strong for fear of the consequences. To maintain the Background, brute power has to be equipotent, and so the boundary of the Background is to be found at the limits of brute equipotency.

In a way, this conclusion is unsurprising, because brute equipotency is the social equivalent of the equipollence prized by the ancient Sceptics. For them, equipollence meant 'equality with regard to being convincing: [so that] none of the conflicting accounts take precedence over any other as being more convincing'.[98] With social scepticism, we are concerned with the social construction of the world, and that does not require the creation of equipollent deontic powers because it will be more deontologically parsimonious if the original ones are simply weakened or eliminated. But that cannot be all. The elimination of deontic powers depends on brute equipotency. Just as the natural world is made by brute facts, the social one is ultimately made by brute power, and to remain in a state of deontological inertia a society has to act to ensure that the brute powers of those within it are equivalent, i.e., interchangeable in their capacity to influence the mind against our will. Any inequity in either brute power or in opposing impressions or accounts will inevitably incline the mind one way rather than another. So deontological parsimony entails brute equipotency in the same way as scepticism requires equipollence, and a society can remain deontologically inert only through the continual redistribution of brute power.

If scepticism means enjoying the tranquillity that comes from keeping opposite views in balance so that there is nothing that predominates and compels judgement, this outcome can be achieved in a socially realized scepticism only by eliminating both deontic powers and the imbalance of brute forces that gives rise to them. Just as the outcome of scepticism is an egalitarian mental world, the outcome of social scepticism is an egalitarian social world. You can't dispel brute power by thinking about it, any more than you can think away the dog's bite, but collective intention, or rather the lack of it, does undermine the brute force of deontic power because, unlike dogs, social bodies only have teeth because we have supplied them. Scepticism brutalizes power, but it does not have to lead to the war of all against all. If it results in the balance of equipotent forces presupposed in the Background, it may produce not just mental tranquillity but social harmony as well.

Deontological inertia

We now have something like an account of the social generated from within scepticism. Social scepticism is a form of collective (in)action that results in a more deontologically parsimonious world. Its key elements are the brute equipotency of its (deontologically prodigal) agents, and their social coordination without deontology, i.e., dealienation. One definition of alienation might be this. Through the collective intentions of others or, indeed, of oneself with others, it is impossible to live naturally in the world. In a deontologically parsimonious world it should be possible to live both socially and naturally.

However, deontological parsimony is always a relative concept: a state of affairs is deontologically parsimonious relative to the way it was before or the way it might have been. So there are innumerable forms of social (in)action that might prove to be somewhat deontologically parsimonious in effect, whether by accident or design or some combination of the two. The social exists wherever there is deontologically parsimonious social complexity, and the question of how to insert a socially complex, and therefore potentially deontically prodigal, society into a less complex, more deontically inert environment is one that can be iterated at many levels both within and between human societies.

Social complexity, which generates many instrumental powers even when it is not generating deontic powers, is liable to undermine brute equipotency with any less complex social environment with which it is in contact. Whenever this occurs there is always the danger that relative social complexity will create brute inequalities. Those in turn may generate new deontic powers which, though made within the space of complexity, are exercised outside it – in other words, outside the sphere of brute equipotency which sustains internal deontological parsimony. It is therefore theoretically possible for a society to be at the same time deontologically parsimonious within its own boundaries, but deontologically prodigal in its dealings with those outside. One way to avoid this is to ensure brute equipotency between more complex social forms and their less complex environments.

With the habitual instrumentalization of brute equipotency, the world becomes increasingly deontologically inert until it approximates to the Background, where everyone acts solely from natural inclination and anyone can correct anyone else. However, although all of the Background is deontologically inert, the social is just a subset of the Background, for the deeper you go into the Background the more it converges with nature itself. And this raises an important question. Even the most deontologically parsimonious human world is liable to be less deontologically inert than the natural world around it. Among the species that we know, it is human beings alone who through language and action create the complex systems of external rules and powers that govern their interaction with each other. For all the wolf packs and whale pods and termite colonies that might be found in it, the natural world without *Homo sapiens* is going to be far more deontologically parsimonious than any world with humans in it. In consequence, nature will become alienated from itself in a world shaped by human deontic powers, so that even if not directly the subject of those powers, it becomes alienated from its natural context and functioning.

It is obvious that only a deontologically neutral society is compatible with a deontologically neutral ecology, for any society is a constituent part of a wider ecology. But being internally parsimonious does not guarantee external parsimony, particularly if the society in question is socially complex enough to exercise brute power over its environment, because brute power is quickly translated into the deontic power required to perpetuate it. It is therefore possible for a society to be internally dealienated, but nevertheless alienating to its natural (as well as its social) environment. In the case of human beings, that alienation is registered in the concept of the Anthropocene. Although not itself a set of deontic powers, the Anthropocene is the geophysical index of the exercise of deontic rather than brute powers, the way that nature re-presents itself not as it is made by nature but as it is remade through deontic powers. As such it provides a perfect example of the way something natural, the human species, may through deontic power create a controlling and alien environment both for itself and for other forms of life.

Without humans, there is no world to speak of; it is all Background. It would therefore seem to follow that, as almost the sole creators and bearers of deontic powers, humans should exclude themselves from the biosphere just as other deontically prodigal imbalances of brute power are excluded. For the thoroughgoing sceptic, such a world would perhaps be the one most clearly consistent with their scepticism. Where opposition to alienation is derived from scepticism rather than (as it is in the early Marx) humanism, there can be no objection to human extinction per se. A sceptic cannot fault a species reduced to extinction by its own uncertainty. Indeed it has a certain piquancy. Buridan's ass showed the way. But while there is no logical reason not to embrace this *reductio*, accepting the possibility of human extinction with equanimity does not answer the apraxia challenge. To accept that a world without humans would be OK, is also to accept that a world without sceptics would be OK, but a world without sceptics is one with no place for a sceptic to live, so the charge that it is impossible to live as a sceptic has renewed force.

The first question scepticism poses for politics is therefore that of how a deontologically parsimonious society can be inserted into a deontologically inert natural environment without becoming deontologically prodigal. This is the problem that even mild to moderate scepticism forces the political theorist to address before any other, because without an answer to it there is no excuse for human societies at all. Can the problems of both internal and external deonticity be remedied simultaneously?[99] Let's suppose that scepticism provides an argument for a more deontologically parsimonious world, and that communism and posthumanism are two of the worlds it might provide arguments for. Even if a post-anthropic communism were to reverse the effects of capitalism, that would still account for only part of the alienating power that humans have taken over nature.[100] Deontological parsimony precludes war against other species, just as it does war against other tribes or nations, so from this perspective the Anthropocene extends back as far as the extinction of the megafauna. A form of human society alienating neither to itself nor to the nature of which it is a part would have no deontic footprint and no deontically derived powers either within or between species.

Is this possible? How can even a deontologically parsimonious human world be accommodated within deontically inert nature without assuming deontic powers over it? At the end of *The World Without Us*, a description of a world from which humans have disappeared, Alan Weisman talks to a scientist who fantasizes about using lasers or particle-wave beams to build things remotely on other planets, including human beings, and remarks: 'If we could do that — find a fertile planet somewhere big enough for all of us, holographically clone our bodies, and upload our minds across light-years — eventually the Earth would do fine without us.'[101] In an ideal world of scepticism, the social would be made through the deontological equivalent of this procedure. It would involve reengineering human society to become a deontologically inert simulacrum of the social world that already exists. If that were achievable, it would make no difference if that society were physically located on another planet or on this one. The existence of human society would not have an alienating effect on the rest of nature.

Perhaps the social, the unintended anomic space that emerges within society in modernity, provides a model not just for how the whole of human society might be, but for how human society might be within and relative to nature, in which case the social could be recast as a bivalent concept: although it emerges as an anomic space in an otherwise nomic complex society, it could also describe a space of social complexity in an otherwise anomic nature, so that the same socially complex but anomic space simultaneously functions as the exception in both contexts. If so, it provides a model answer to the question of how a human society might be accommodated within nature in a deontologically parsimonious way. It could be the result of the nomic becoming anomic or the natural becoming more socially complex or the conjunction of the two, provided there is continuous deontological inertia at the point of contact or across the area of their overlap.

With continuous deontological inertia, it should be possible to move back and forth across the culture–nature boundary without noticing. Achieved through the instrumentalization of deontic powers, this movement should result in what Durkheim calls the 'gentle dénouement' of the struggle for existence in which rivals 'can co-exist side by side' thanks to specialization.[102] But where that is impossible, then, where two deontically neutral worlds are adjacent or overlapping, there will be continuity between them only if they are equipotent at the point of contact; otherwise the one with more brute power will start, if deontically prodigal, to alienate the other.

Brute equipotency in a deontologically inert environment potentially allows anyone to correct anyone else, just as in the Background. In the space of overlap between the human and animal worlds, this means not eradicating natural threats and accepting that dog bites are just one of the forms such correction might take. However, social scepticism does not entail denying the reality of the dog's bite, merely accepting it as one of the natural hazards of the collectively unillusioned life, and of living in an interspecific Background. Social scepticism is not disproved when the world bites back; being bitten is one of the contingencies it anticipates, because it might be one of the ways that deontological inertia is maintained. That's how brute equipotency works, and the resulting pain provides some reassurance that it has been achieved.

The concept of the social suggests that, rather than being an irrefutable but untenable philosophical position, scepticism has a viable social form, and that it can provide a basis for accepting the consequences of the global deontological inertia it entails. Those consequences might sometimes feel uncomfortable, but they are not unliveable.

2
Vectors of the Biopolitical

Man is by nature a political animal

Aristotle, *Politics*

From one sentence in Aristotle derive two arresting theoretical discourses of the twenty-first century: Michel Foucault's biopolitics, provocatively reformulated by Giorgio Agamben in terms of the relationship between sovereignty and the body, and the capabilities approach developed by Amartya Sen and Martha Nussbaum as a means of evaluating and promoting development, justice and freedom. Both are characterized by deep reflection on the sources of Western political thought, and by urgent engagement with contemporary social and legal problems. Both are in some sense biopolitical in that they are shaped by the interplay of the same Aristotelian categories – the human and the animal, politics and nature. But they are on opposite sides of the divide that has opened up in the human sciences since the 1960s, and there currently seems no optic through which they might simultaneously be viewed, no way of integrating or comparing their insights.

In part, this reflects a situation in which political debate appears to have fragmented into a multiplicity of single issues. The ancient 'Who will rule?' and the modern 'Who shall have what?' have been supplemented by an array of questions that deal with matters once exclusively cultural, personal or natural. For previous eras, the relative integrity and unmalleability of cultures, bodies and environments rendered such questions redundant. Now they frequently appear unanswerable from within established political traditions, and incommensurable in relation to each other. Within this expanded field, biopolitics and the capabilities approach have unusual salience and potential, for both bundle together issues otherwise assumed to be distinct. If they, in turn, could be coordinated, perhaps we could begin to map the new territory.

Bare life

In the introductory volume of *The History of Sexuality*, Foucault remarked that whereas 'for millennia, man remained what he was for Aristotle: a living animal with the additional capacity for a political existence; modern man is an animal whose politics places his existence as a living being in question'. Rather than being an 'inaccessible substrate' presupposed by political life, the biological life of man had now 'passed into knowledge's field of control and power's sphere of intervention'.[1]

According to Foucault, this occurred through the development of the disciplines of the body and the regulation

of the population. The first of these focused on the individual human body, increasing its usefulness and economic
integration through 'the optimization of its capabilities';
the second on the collective body: 'births and mortality,
the level of health, life expectancy and longevity' and the
environmental variables that controlled them.[2] The result
was that the animal life of man, far from being irrelevant
to politics, now became its subject, 'a kind of bestialization
of man achieved through the most sophisticated political
techniques'.[3]

Taking his cue from Arendt, Agamben argues that political existence and bestialized life represent distinct types of
being.[4] For the Greeks, he claims, *zōē* was the term for the
natural life of nutrition and reproduction shared with other
living creatures, while *bios* was used to describe ways of
living a distinctively human life:

> When Plato mentions three kinds of life in the *Philebus*, and when
> Aristotle distinguishes the contemplative life of the philosopher
> (*bios theōrētikos*) from the life of pleasure (*bios apolaustikos*) and
> the political life (*bios politikos*) in the *Nicomachean Ethics*, neither
> philosopher would ever have used the term *zōē* … to speak of a *zōē*
> *politikē* of the citizens of Athens would have made no sense.[5]

The difference between political life and the 'simple fact
of living' is therefore grounded in the underlying distinction between *bios* and *zōē*. It is in this light that we must
read Aristotle's assertion that although the polis 'comes into
existence for the sake of life, it exists for the good life':[6] The
polis may have originated in the need to secure 'bare life',

mere human survival, but that is no longer what it is for. Simple natural life 'is excluded from the polis in the strict sense and remains confined – as merely reproductive life – to the sphere of the *oikos*, "home"'.[7]

From its inception, the fundamental binaries of Western political thought are those of 'bare life/political existence, *zōē/bios*, exclusion/inclusion'. The transition described by Foucault is therefore an event of world historical importance, and 'the entry of *zōē* into the sphere of the polis ... the decisive event of modernity'. However, whereas Foucault understood the animal life of man to have become the subject/object of biopower primarily through the development of nineteenth-century discourses and disciplines of the body, Agamben posits an alternative source at the 'hidden point of intersection between the juridico-institutional and the biopolitical models of power'.[8]

Following Schmitt, Agamben argues that the sovereign is he who decides the exception, and reincludes within the law precisely what had been excluded from it, namely the state of nature. *Zōē*, not *bios*, is the form of life characteristic of the state of nature, so in the state of exception the sovereign effects the reinclusion of 'bare life' within the polis. Since sovereignty is exhaustively defined by its ability to decide the exception, it follows that 'the inclusion of bare life in the political realm constitutes the original – if concealed – nucleus of sovereign power. *It can even be said that the production of a biopolitical body is the original activity of sovereign power.*'[9]

Agamben makes no distinction between the private and the political, on the one hand, and nature and culture on the other. For him, 'the fundamental activity of sovereign power is the production of bare life as originary political element and as threshold of articulation between nature and culture, *ʒōē* and *bios*.' The implications of this are elaborated in terms of the Aristotelian distinction between voice (expressive forms of communication shared with animals) and language (the rational communication needed to establish justice in the polis). Arguing that 'the question "In what way does the living being have language?" corresponds exactly to the question "In what way does bare life dwell in the polis?"', Agamben suggests that the state of exception is characterized by the production of life-forms deprived of communication.[10]

A model is provided by the nineteenth-century biologist Ernst Haeckel, who postulated an ape-man without speech, *Homo alalus*, as the evolutionary ancestor of *Homo sapiens*. In what sense would the non-speaking man be a man rather than an ape? Is it not simply a matter of positing a creature already fully human and then depriving it of speech? In the same way, the state of exception 'functions by excluding as not (yet) human an already human being from itself, that is, by animalizing the human'.[11]

This move clarifies and expands the range of life forms potentially created by sovereign power. Not just the *homo alalus*, or ape-man, but also the *Muselmann*, the hopeless victim of the concentration camps, the neomort and the over-comatose person. Above all, sovereignty creates outlaws such as the *homo sacer*, the 'sacred' outlaw of ancient Rome, whom all were free to kill with impunity. The life of the outlaw 'is pure *ʒōē*',[12] and so the exclusion of a human from the polis is equivalent to the inclusion of bare life within it – a doubling represented in the archetypal figure of the werewolf:

> a monstrous hybrid of human and animal, divided between the forest and the city – the werewolf – is, therefore, in its origin the figure of the man who has been banned from the city ... The life of the bandit, like that of the sacred man, is not a piece of animal nature without any relation to law and the city. It is, rather, a threshold of indistinction and of passage between animal and man.[13]

Where, as in contemporary politics, exception becomes increasingly the norm, 'the realm of bare life – which is originally situated at the margins of the political order – gradually begins to coincide with the political realm' and exclusion and inclusion, *bios* and *ʒōē* enter into 'a zone of irreducible indistinction'. Then 'all citizens can be said ... to appear virtually as *homines sacri*'.[14]

Capabilities

Amartya Sen first turned to Aristotle for a very different reason: to free himself from the utilitarian emphasis on a single aggregate measure of utility. Aristotle reminds us that pleasures may be as distinct as the activities involved, so even if we were to take pleasure as the only measure we would still be left with pleasures of incommensurable kinds. Nevertheless, Sen argued, the resulting plurality may be constitutive rather than competitive, provided we think of utility as a vector with several distinct components.[15]

On this basis, he began to recast his account of plural utility, arguing that individual circumstances and life-achievements might be considered as functionings that could be combined into a 'functioning vector'. A person's potential functioning vectors would then constitute a capability set, which could provide a context-sensitive basis for comparison of standards of living and interpersonal equality.[16] Only later did it dawn on Sen that his account of capabilities had 'something in common' with Aristotle's analysis of human functions in which 'the good of man resides in the function of man'.[17]

It was Martha Nussbaum who elaborated the Aristotelian basis of this project, and found the proof text needed to link Sen's conception of plural utility with the Aristotelian conception of the role of the state: 'It is evident that the best *politeia* is that arrangement according to which anyone whatsoever might do best and live a flourishing life.'[18] Interpreting 'arrangement' (*taxis*) to mean a theory of distributive justice, 'anyone whatsoever' (*hostisoun*) to include 'each and every member of the community', and a 'flourishing life' (*zoië makariōs*) to encompass both whatever functions are specific to a particular individual, and those generally needed for a full life, Nussbaum was able to gloss this as 'an Aristotelian conception of the proper function of government, according to which its task is to make available to each and every member of the community the basic necessary conditions of the capability to choose and live a fully good human life, with respect to each of the major functions included in that fully good life'.[19]

But what is a good human life? Does the human being as such actually have a function or activity? According to Aristotle, the mere act of living appears to be shared even by plants, whereas we are looking to the function peculiar to man; we must therefore set aside the life of nutrition and growth. Next in the scale will come some form of sentient life; but this too seems to be shared by horses, oxen and animals generally. There remains therefore what may be called the practical life of that which has reason.[20]

Seen in this light, there are, Nussbaum argues, 'two distinct thresholds: a threshold of capability to function beneath which a life will be so impoverished that it will not be human at all; and a somewhat higher threshold, beneath which those characteristic functions are available in such a reduced way that, though we may judge the form of life a human one, we will not think it a *good* human life'.[21] The task of the city is 'to effect the transition from one level of capability to another', from mere life to human life, and from human life to the good life. In the latter case, because 'the human being is by nature a political being', the city is more than instrumental, for Aristotle makes 'the self-sufficiency involved in human *eudaimonia* a communal and not a solitary self-sufficiency'.[22]

In practice, therefore, achieving a threshold means making a social transition. For women, with whom Nussbaum was concerned in a UN-sponsored project in the late 1980s and early 1990s, this might involve working outside the family house, a major issue in societies where women are traditionally prohibited from doing so, even when survival is at stake. Here, the transition is from the 'private realm, or the home, in which people do things out of love and affection rather than mutual respect' to the 'public realm, characterized by reciprocity among rough equals'. But as women leave the family to enter the public realm, the public realm also means 'acknowledging that the family is a political institution, not part of a "private sphere" immune from justice'.[23]

But if, for women, reaching a threshold means a transition from the private to the political, Nussbaum is also keen to shift the emphasis of 'political animal' back towards the animal. Emphasizing that for Sen, too, 'the bodily capabilities and functionings are intrinsically good and not … *merely* instrumental means to other higher goods', Nussbaum argues that the Aristotelian conception of the human being as a 'political animal' means viewing a human as someone 'who has an animal body and whose human dignity, rather than being opposed to this animal nature, inheres in it, and in its temporal trajectory'.[24]

This applies not just to the animal life of humanity but to non-human animals as well. Kant might think 'human dignity and our moral capacity … radically separate from the natural world', but Aristotle saw 'considerable continuity between human capacity and the capacities of other animals'. For Nussbaum, human need has to include 'our animal neediness and animal capacities', and we have to acknowledge that 'our dignity just is the dignity of a certain sort of animal'.[25]

To achieve a threshold of animal capacity or dignity may imply a different type of transition. For many of the cases discussed in *Frontiers of Justice*, in which Nussbaum extends the scope of the capabilities approach to those of differing abilities, nationality or species, the transition does not involve entering the public realm. Some of those with impairments and disabilities 'could not be included in the group of political choosers, however generously we assess their potential', but if their capabilities link them 'to the human community rather than some other', they may nevertheless reach a threshold of human life.[26]

Although, for other species, political functionings fall outside the species norm, that does not mean that the capabilities of other species can be sustained within nature. Species sovereignty is one ideal, but for most animals it is simply not a possibility; for dogs, for example, there is usually 'no option to flourish in an all-dog community; their community is always one that includes intimate human members'. In any case, 'we cannot just leave nature alone and expect it to manage itself', for 'nature is not just, and species are not all nice'. The capabilities approach cannot be realized in the wild or without human intervention. It requires wheelchairs to be made for disabled Alsatians, and 'the intelligent and careful use of zoos and animal parks', for only in such places can non-human animals realize their capabilities without mutual harm.[27]

Vectors

For both Nussbaum and Agamben, the essential dichotomy is between the good life, or the political life, and the life that is, for whatever reason, lacking in those qualities. Like Aristotle, both emphasize that this amounts to the difference between what is distinctively human and what is less than fully human. Aristotle had argued that anyone who lives a life of pleasure is, in effect, 'choosing the life of dumb grazing animals', and that anyone who is perpetually asleep, or comatose, is living the life of a vegetable.[28] Nussbaum suggests that failure to allow a basic capability to develop is to condemn whoever possesses it to 'a kind of premature death, the death of a form of flourishing', while Agamben offers an entire bestiary of bare life extending all the way to a tick that lived in a laboratory for many years without movement or nutrition.[29]

But if, for Agamben, bare life is the hopeless destination towards which the logic of modernity points, for Nussbaum it is the base from which capabilities are expanded and joyfully transformed into functionings. The polarities appear to be the same, but the directions different. If so, is there some point at which human flourishing and bestialization meet, some limbo in which the half-dead pass those whose capabilities have been brought to life?

One way to establish this is to take coordinates from Aristotle. The passage that is central to both Nussbaum and Agamben reads as follows:

> It is clear that the city-state is a natural growth, and that man is by nature a political animal, and a man that is by nature and not merely by fortune citiless is either low in the scale of humanity [an inferior being] or above it (like the 'clanless, lawless, hearthless' man reviled by Homer ...) inasmuch as he resembles an isolated piece at draughts. And why man is a political animal in a greater measure than any bee or any gregarious animal is clear. For nature, as we declare, doth nothing without purpose; and man alone of all the animals possesses speech [*logos*]. The mere voice, it is true, can indicate pain or pleasure, and therefore is possessed by the other

animals as well (for their nature has been developed so far as to have sensations of what is painful and pleasant and signify these sensations to one another), but speech is designed to indicate the advantageous and the harmful, and therefore also the right and the wrong; for it is the special property of man in distinction from the other animals that he alone has perception of good and bad and right and wrong and the other moral qualities, and it is partnership in these things that makes a household and a city-state.[30]

In this famous and much-debated passage, which follows an account of the evolution of ever-larger aggregations of humanity, from the couple to the city-state, Aristotle implicitly defines the *zōon politikon* in terms of two variables that are at least conceptually distinguishable. On the one hand there is natural gregariousness, which is opposed to natural solitude, and on the other, there is *logos*, which is opposed to voice.

Gregariousness, as Aristotle explains elsewhere, is just a matter of flocking together, and as such is common to land, air and sea creatures of many species. Solitary animals may include man himself, people like the outlaw described by Homer. In contrast, the distinction between voice and *logos* is a measure of what distinguishes the human from the animal. So, not all gregarious animals have rational speech, and not everyone that has speech is gregarious.

The implied relationship between Aristotle's taxonomic categories is often unclear, but the *logos*–voice axis is perhaps better thought of as intersecting with the gregarious –solitary axis than as a subdivision or extension of it. When Aristotle says that humans are more political than bees, he does not mean that they are more gregarious, but rather that they have some other quality as well. Political animals are distinguished from the merely gregarious by having a common activity. Examples include 'man, bees, wasps, ants, cranes', some of which live under a ruler and some of which do not.[31] What makes gregarious animals political is a shared way of life to which all contribute, and what makes humans even more political is having *logos*, for rational communication permits common activity of greater social and moral complexity.

Within the terrain mapped by Aristotle's definition of the political animal, there would therefore appear to be two axes: one that extends from solitude to gregariousness, and from the private to the public, and another that extends from voice to *logos*, or nature to culture. Using these axes, it becomes possible to plot with more precision the vectors described by Agamben and Nussbaum, both in relation to Aristotle and to each other.

Foucault was primarily concerned with the axis that leads from the private to the public, and with a double imbrication brought about through the regulation of bodies and populations – simultaneously an encroachment of the private upon the public and the public upon the private. Agamben turns Foucault's vector of privatization towards naturalization by interpreting the private–public axis in terms of the *ʒōē/bios* distinction; and (through the equation of *ʒōē* with speechlessness) by enhancing the literalness of Foucault's 'bestialization of man'. The reorientation is completed when Agamben shifts the emphasis to sovereign power. Hobbes, he argues, does not think of the state of nature as a prehistoric epoch, but as a 'principle internal to the State revealed in the moment in which the State is considered "as if it were dissolved"'. In the state of nature, man is wolf to man, so 'this lupization of man and humanization of the wolf is at every moment possible in the *dissolutio civitatis* inaugurated by the state of exception'.[32]

A *dissolutio civitatis* might be expected to effect a return to the private realm, for Agamben claims to be working with 'the classical distinction between ζōē and *bios*, between private life and political existence, between man as a simple living being at home in the house and man's political existence in the city'.[33] But although he places bare life 'in the no-man's land between the home and the city' it is apparent that in his examples of men exiled from the city, the outlaw does not retire to enjoy a private life with his family.[34] The werewolf is to be found between 'the forest and the city', not half-way between the polis and the *oikos*.

Nussbaum takes as her starting point Rousseau's memorable picture of bare life ('All are born naked and poor. All are subject to the miseries of life …'), and argues that 'people are entitled not only to mere life, but to a life compatible with human dignity'.[35] Because man is political, acquiring human dignity involves projecting the alienated, the private and the ungregarious into the public realm, and because man is an animal this means that his animal needs and animal dignity find their satisfaction in the public realm as well. Initially at least, Nussbaum is working primarily with the private–public axis, where she describes a vector which (like Foucault's 'optimization of the capabilities of the body') travels from bare life towards the public sphere.

However, because animal dignity is of a kind shared by non-human animals as well, the optimization of non-human capabilities also inscribes a trajectory that leads not so much from private to public as from nature to culture. And in *Frontiers of Justice* she switches her attention to the other axis. Rather as the *homo sacer* does not go home but ends up becoming part of nature instead, the animal whose capabilities are developed participates in culture rather than politics. Although each takes something like a ninety-degree turn, the trajectories described by Nussbaum and Agamben continue to be opposing vectors: Agamben's equation of the *dissolutio civitatis* with the state of nature allows bare life to take on animal form, while Nussbaum, translating animal dignity into the dignity of animals, brings nature into the sphere of culture.

There is, it seems, no one route to the biopolitical, only converging vectors of privatization, naturalization, acculturation and socialization. But what is the unknown region into which political exiles, werewolves, Alsatians in wheelchairs and working women all now wearily make their way?

The absent centre
In Aristotle, both the solitary–gregarious and the voice–*logos* axes are continuous and have a discernible, if poorly defined, middle ground. Between solitude and the gregariousness of the city, there are first couples, then households, then villages. Those who inhabit the middle of the range are to a greater or lesser degree scattered, a condition shared by Cyclopes and ground larks, among other creatures.[36] Between voice and *logos* there are intermediate states as

well. The slave 'participates in reason so far as to apprehend it but not to possess it' and lacks the deliberative part of the soul; women have the deliberative part but without full authority; children possess it in undeveloped form.[37]

These two axes meet in the household, which is about half-way between solitude and gregariousness, and potentially incorporates all the states between *logos* and voice – the master, the wife, the slave, the ox.[38] Aristotle admitted that 'man is not only a political but also a domestic animal [*oikonomikon ζōon*]', and at the intersection of the axes this is what all would appear to become.[39] Yet Aristotle could not conceive of a household without a master, or a situation in which households alone could occupy anything other than a discontinuous social space. The middle ground is there, but sparsely populated.

So what happens when man becomes, biopolitically, a domestic animal? Agamben points to 'a zone of indifference … within which – like a "missing link" which is always lacking because it is already virtually present – the articulation between human and animal, man and non-man, speaking being and living being, must take place. Like every space of exception, this zone is, in truth, perfectly empty'.[40]

But the void has a name, for it is what Arendt (whose argument in *The Human Condition* Agamben otherwise follows quite closely) calls society, or 'the social'. In antiquity, the household 'was the sphere where the necessities of life … were taken care of', and in the modern world society is a sort of 'national household', in which 'mutual dependence for the sake of life and nothing else assumes public

significance and where the activities connected with sheer
survival are permitted to appear in public'.[41]

This 'national household' or 'society' is also conceived in
Aristotelian terms, though Arendt reinterprets both axes in
her own way. The axis which leads from solitude to gregariousness, the private to the public, is defined by the polarities
of labour and action. Labour includes and supports the biological processes of the human body, and does not need the
presence of others; action, as 'the only activity that goes on
directly between men without the intermediary of things or
matter', is 'entirely dependent upon the constant presence
of others'.[42]

Action alone constitutes the *bios politikos*, and a life
without it 'has ceased to be a human life because it is no
longer lived among men', like the life of the *animal laborans* who is 'imprisoned in the privacy of his own body'.[43]
But modernity has seen the triumph of the *animal laborans*,
as economic and technological advance has freed mankind
from necessity, and brought the private activities of production and consumption into the public realm, replacing it
with a 'consumers' society'.

Alongside this, Arendt develops a distinctive account
of the other axis in which the opposites are represented by
'the world', which is 'the human artefact, the fabrication of
human hands', and 'the earth or nature'. The earth 'provides
human beings with a habitat in which they can move and
breathe', but through work, as opposed to labour, is formed
'an "artificial" world of things, distinctly different from all
natural surroundings'. Work is therefore the activity 'which
corresponds to the unnaturalness of human existence'; it

separates man from his environment, even though 'life itself is outside this artificial world, and through life man remains related to all other living organisms'.[44]

Human life, in so far as it is world-building, is engaged in reification, but scientific doubt and secularization undermine the perceived permanence and value of culture, and so humans become separated from the world that they have created. In 'world alienation' it is 'as though we had forced open the distinguishing boundaries which protected the world, the human artifice, from nature' and all that is left are 'appetites and desires, the senseless urges of [man's] body'. In this state, whatever was 'not necessitated by life's metabolism with nature, was either superfluous or could be justified only in terms of a peculiarity of human as distinguished from other animal life'.[45] Here, language becomes voice, and culture returns to nature.

On both axes there is a double movement. Modernity has been both world-alienating and earth-alienating, as the abstractions of science and technology have distanced man from the earth. At the same time, 'the final stage in the disappearance of the public realm' has been accompanied by the 'liquidation of the private realm', the two realms 'constantly flow into each other like waves in the never-resting stream of the life-process itself' until 'the submersion of both in the sphere of the social'.[46]

Into the maelstrom

For Arendt, the vectors of the biopolitical form the vortex of the social. But as she recoiled from the maelstrom, she watched others behold it with equanimity. In particular,

Marx, who, she claimed, transformed the vortex of modernity into a political programme. The 'withering away of the public realm' in which the state gives way to pure administration was the prelude to Marx's 'withering away of the state'. Marx did not, indeed, could not have known that 'the germs of communistic society were present in the reality of a national household', but 'a complete victory of society will always produce some sort of "communistic fiction", whose outstanding political characteristic is that it is indeed ruled by an invisible hand'.[47]

Conversely, Marx's 'socialization of man' embodied the opposing vector. It could be achieved by revolutionary expropriation, but 'a slower and no less certain "withering away" of the private realm in general and of private property in particular' was already underway, as the private became increasingly political. For example, 'the fact that the modern age emancipated the working classes and the women at nearly the same historical moment must certainly be counted among the characteristics of an age which no longer believes that bodily functions and material functions should be hidden'.[48]

Arendt's identification of Marxism with modernity was intended as a critique of both. Yet Sen and Nussbaum make what amounts to the same claim when they insist that the capabilities approach 'takes its start from the Aristotelian/Marxian conception of the human being as a social and political being, who finds fulfilment in relations with others'.[49] Nussbaum argues that 'the basic intuitive idea of my version of the capabilities approach is ... a life that has available in it "truly human functioning" in the sense described by

Marx',[50] and she repeatedly uses a quotation from Marx as an epigraph:

> It will be seen how in place of the *wealth* and *poverty* of political economy come the *rich human being* and the rich human need. The *rich* human being is simultaneously the human being *in need of* a totality of human-life activities – the man in whom his own realization exists as an inner necessity, as *need*.[51]

The passage in question describes the transformed life of man under communism, and Nussbaum explicitly equates 'truly human functioning' with this condition. Acknowledging that 'the *sense* caught up in crude practical need has only a *restricted* sense', Marx had argued in the 'Economic and Philosophical Manuscripts' that 'it is obvious that the *human* eye gratifies itself in a way different from the crude non-human eye; the human *ear* from the crude ear'. It is precisely this transformation that is involved in the transition from basic capabilities to full functioning. According to Nussbaum, the central task of the city is not to take care of people's 'perceptual needs in a mechanical way, producing a seeing eye, a hearing ear, etc'; it is rather to 'make it possible for people to use their bodies and their senses in a truly human way'.[52]

Similar alignments between Marxist thought and the vectors of the biopolitical are to be found on the nature–culture axis. According to Arendt, 'world alienation' is the equivalent of Marx's dealienation, in which man reappropriates cultural production as a species being. It was Marx who likened Milton to a silkworm, and in the Marxist utopia, where all may write poetry on this basis, 'world alienation is even more present than it was before'.[53] Agamben makes the same point, quoting Kojève's version of the 'Hegelo-Marxist end of history', where 'men would construct their edifices and works of art as birds build their nests and spiders spin their webs, and would perform musical concerts after the fashion of frogs and cicadas'.[54] And it is, of course, Marx's claim that 'communism as completed naturalism is humanism and as completed humanism is naturalism'[55] that is knowingly echoed in Agamben's statement that the 'lupization of man and humanization of the wolf is at every moment possible in the *dissolutio civitatis*'.

Valences of the social

Although the vectors of the biopolitical are plotted in Aristotelian terms, their trajectories are derived not so much from Aristotle as from Marx's reading of him. It is as though Marx's early vision of communism had been bisected, with Agamben taking up his account of depoliticization and naturalization, and Nussbaum his vision of socialization and humanization. But if biopolitics and capabilities represent two halves of Marx's totalizing theory, can they also be reunited to describe a single movement?

Not necessarily, for the fragments have acquired widely differing valences: Sen and Nussbaum present the capabilities approach as being equivalent to (and perhaps a substitute for) the projected path of human development envisioned by communism; while for Arendt and Agamben, the logic of modernity is identical with that which leads to totalitarianism and the camps. At one point, Agamben comes close to describing the convergence of all the vectors: 'For a humanity that has become animal again, there is nothing left but the depoliticization of human societies by means of the unconditioned unfolding of the *oikonomia*, or the taking on of biological life itself as the supreme political (or rather impolitical) task.' He acknowledges its imaginative location in Kojève's end of history, but finds its historical realization in 'the totalitarianisms of the twentieth century'.[56]

Something of this duality is already present in Marx. When read in the light of Aristotle's definition of the political animal, it becomes apparent that states of alienation and communism are created in a similar way. Marx himself acknowledges that the alienated man of civil society is the closest approximation to the socialized political animal of Aristotle:

> Only in the eighteenth century, in 'civil society', do the various forms of social connectedness confront the individual as a mere means towards his private purposes, as external necessity. But the epoch which produces this standpoint, that of the isolated individual, is also precisely that of the hitherto most developed social (from this standpoint, general) relations. The human being is in the most literal sense a *ζῷον πολιτικόν* [political animal], not merely a gregarious animal, but an animal which can individuate itself only in the midst of society.[57]

The parallel is unsurprising, for both alienation and communism are defined within the same matrix, one axis of which locates man's simultaneous alienation from nature and from his own cultural production, the other his alienation from both public and private life. Marx's early references to alienation allude to one or another of these forms of estrangement: 'alienated labour tears man from the object of his production ... his own body, nature exterior to him, and his intellectual being, his human essence'.[58] Together they constitute alienation from species-being, the life that man would have if he were fully socialized, and if society was not merely the means but also the end.

If alienation has at least a fourfold form – from culture and from nature, and from the private and the political – so too does dealienation. Communism involves 'the positive abolition of all alienation, thus the return of man out of religion, family, state, etc [he might have added, nature], into his human, i.e. social being'.[59] It takes place both on the public–private axis, where 'human emancipation will only be complete when the real, individual man has absorbed into himself the abstract citizen; when as an individual man, in his everyday life, in his work, and in his relationships, he has become a *species-being*'; and on that of nature and culture: 'society completes the essential unity of man and nature ... the accomplished naturalism of man and the accomplished humanism of nature'.[60]

What then constitutes the difference between communism and alienation? Are they, as Arendt implied, just alternative ways of describing the same thing? Marx presents the vectors of the biopolitical as part of an ambiguous totality. Alienation and communism happen in the same place, in that both are the product of the same vectors. However, in the former, only man has been transformed, as he moves away from static polarities; in the latter, the world itself is changed as those polarities draw together. The alienated human beings of civil society are prematurely social, living in society before the socialization of the world.

Within this context, communism is an act of restoration, 'a *restoration* of the human world and of human relationships to *man himself*'. For example, in civil society man is on the one hand 'a member of civil society … and on the other a citizen', and there is a gap between the two that is closed when 'individual man has absorbed into himself the abstract citizen'.[61] This involves not so much the transformation of the individual as the transformation of the world through the withering away of the state. Similarly, whereas for Nussbaum, the transition from animal seeing to human sight is effected through the transformation of the individual, and the social functions only as the means to that transformation, Marx envisaged something different. For him, 'the human character of the senses … can only come into being through the existence of *its* object, through humanized nature'; the eye becomes 'a *human* eye when its *object* has become a *human*, social object' and this occurs only when 'he himself becomes a social being and society becomes a being for him in this object'.[62] The difference between the capabilities approach and the Marxist project it seeks to realize here becomes apparent, for moving from bare capability to fully human functioning is alienating just in so far as it is not universal.

The same applies to other vectors of the biopolitical. One man excluded from the public realm is disenfranchised, when all are excluded the public realm has disappeared; the zoo animal is alienated from nature in a way that the domestic animal is not; one woman who escapes the confines of the family is distanced from private life, a large voluntary female labour force is not; we cannot all be *homines sacri*: the solitary werewolf may be alienated from his culture, but when we all become werewolves there is no more wolf and no more man. Vehicles of both alienation and of dealienation, the vectors of the biopolitical also provide the measure of each in terms of their differential distribution of a population.

Not everyone is likely to welcome equally the dissolution of politics, the acculturation of nature, the politicization of private life and the naturalization of culture, though most will recognize the relevant vectors within their environment. Less obvious, perhaps, is the extent to which such vectors are enacting a single movement that defines the social space of modernity – the degree of their convergence the index of society. And yet there is no vanishing point – a disenfranchised man does not become a simian citizen, nor a working woman a werewolf – only a diminishing space of contestation, where all try to live the good life, together.

Reuniting the vectors potentially provides a means of articulating the politics of this conceptually expanded but biopolitically contracting field. In particular, it allows us to distinguish, in ways that Marx did not, the state of being equally social from that of being socially equal: the first is measured by convergence between vectors, the second by distributions effected by them. For an egalitarian at least, it may be useful to differentiate non-social equalities – of citizens, members of a family, of animals in nature – from the specifically social equalities that are a function of distances travelled and numbers left behind. To be equally social and socially equal may be utopian, but seeking to measure progress in that direction is not.

3
The Limits of Multitude

How can a blind multitude, which often does not know what it wants ...
undertake so vast and difficult an enterprise as a system of legislation?

Rousseau, *The Social Contract*

The worst of all the multitude
Did something for the common good

Mandeville, *The Grumbling Hive*

Within contemporary politics, there are a lot of questions to which there are many possible answers, and one question to which there is none. There are innumerable projects for utopian futures (and this book offers another) all of which are, in varying degrees, egalitarian, cosmopolitan, ecologically sustainable and locally responsive, but no solution to the most intractable problem of all: Who is going to make it happen?

Almost all the agencies through which political change was effected in the twentieth century have either disappeared or been seriously weakened. There now appear to be only two forces capable of shaping the contemporary world: market globalization propelled by governments and multi-national corporations, and populist reactions that seek to assert national or communal sovereignty. The same actors are frequently involved in both, oscillating between spectacular but sporadic manifestations of the collective will (e.g., the Brexit vote) and the continuation of social and economic practices that undermine their efficacy. But the two are, in fact, related, in that it is the unwillingness of populations to accept the emergent properties of their own habitual behaviour that necessitates the dramatic protests in the first place. All agents seem trapped within this cycle of unintended effect and ineffectual intent – both the market itself and the inchoate nationalisms and fundamentalisms that seek to control it.

Multitude against the people

Within this landscape, a new political agent has been identified – a potential alternative both to the global market and to the populist responses to it. According to Hardt and Negri, the only basis today for 'political action aimed at transformation and liberation' is the multitude, conceived as 'all those who work under the rule of capital and thus potentially as the class of those who refuse the rule of capital'.[1] However, the multitude is primarily defined not by its rejection of the market, but by its distance from the fictive unities of populism:

The multitude is a multiplicity, a plane of singularities, an open set of relations, which is not homogeneous or identical with itself and bears an indistinct, inclusive relation to those outside of it. The people, in contrast, tends toward identity and homogeneity internally while posing its difference from and excluding what remains outside of it. Whereas the multitude is an inconclusive constituent relation, the people is a constituted synthesis that is prepared for sovereignty. The people provides a single will and action that is independent of and often in conflict with the various wills and actions of the multitude. Every nation must make the multitude into a people.[2]

This reaffirmation of the potentialities of the multitude is presented by Paolo Virno as a reversal of the multitude's historic defeat in the political struggles of the seventeenth century, when the choice between 'people' and 'multitude' was 'forged in the fires of intense clashes'. Multitude was the 'losing term', and the bourgeois state was founded on its repression. The multitude and the people therefore become mutually exclusive possibilities: 'If there are people, there is no multitude; if there is a multitude, there are no people.'[3]

In this narrative (also shared, to differing extents, by Balibar and Montag) Hobbes emerges as 'the Marx of the bourgeoisie', so 'haunted by the fear of the masses and their natural tendency to subversion' that he came to 'detest' the multitude.[4] For him, the multitude is little more than 'a regurgitation of the "state of nature" in civil society'. It 'shuns political unity, resists authority, does not enter into lasting agreements, never attains the *status* of a juridical person because it never transfers its own natural rights to the sovereign'.[5] Hobbes's successor in formulating the ideology of the state against the multitude was Rousseau, for whom 'the unity of the people can be created only through an operation of representation that separates it from the multitude'.[6]

Against this victorious tradition, there is only Spinoza, in whose work there is 'nothing of Hobbes or Rousseau' and who stands 'opposed to Hobbes's doctrine at nearly every point'.[7] For Hobbes, 'unanimity is the essence of the political machine ... For Spinoza unanimity is a problem'.[8] In Spinoza's thought, 'the *multitudo* indicates a *plurality which persists as such* ... without converging into a One ... a permanent form, not an episodic or interstitial form'.[9] His conception of the multitude therefore effectively 'banishes sovereignty from politics', creating in its stead 'a politics of permanent revolution ... in which social stability must always be re-created through a constant reorganization of corporeal life, by means of a perpetual mass mobilization'.[10]

People or faction

The basis for this revolutionary rhetoric is a close but tendentious reading of texts in seventeenth-century political theory. For while it is true that Hobbes makes a distinction between the people and the multitude, the way in which he does so is highly specific, and immediately raises difficulties that he cannot completely resolve. As Hobbes acknowledges, both words are potentially ambiguous.

> The word people hath a double signification. In one sense it signifieth only a number of men, distinguished by the place of their

habitation ... which is no more, but the multitude of those particular persons that inhabit those regions ... In another sense, it signifieth a person civil, that is to say, either one man, or one council, in the will whereof is included and involved the will of every one in particular.[11]

Similarly:

Because multitude is a collective word, it is understood to signify more than one object, so that a multitude of men is the same as many men. Because the word is grammatically singular, it also signifies one thing, namely a multitude.[12]

Hobbes seeks to resolve the confusion by using the word multitude to refer to a plurality of individuals in the same place, and the word people to refer to a civil person. However, the distinction is trickier than it might appear, for the people and the multitude are not distinct or opposing forces; they are actually the same individuals: 'The nature of a commonwealth is that a multitude of citizens both exercises power and is subject to power, but in different senses.' When exercising power, 'the multitude is united into a body politic, and thereby are a people'; but when something is done 'by a people as subjects', it is, in effect, done 'by many individuals at the same time', i.e., by a 'multitude'.[13]

The basis of this definition is agency. For Hobbes, the crucial distinction is that which determines whether an action is performed by a multitude of individuals acting separately or by a people collectively acting as one person. This depends neither on the nature of the action, nor on the number and identity of those responsible for it (which may be identical in both cases) but rather on the way in which agency can be ascribed. A multitude cannot 'make a promise or an agreement, acquire or transfer a right, do, have, possess, and so on, except separately or as individuals'.[14] In contrast: 'A *people* is a single entity, with a *single will*: you can attribute *an act* to it.'[15] According to Hobbes, although a multitude of individuals may act individually, they cannot be said to act collectively unless they have actually agreed to do so beforehand. Hence the need for a contract between the individuals who comprise the multitude. Their actions can only count as the act of one person 'if the same multitude individually agree that the will of some one man or the consenting wills of a majority of themselves is to be taken as the will of all'.[16]

In the *Leviathan*, Hobbes presents this agreement as akin to that in which someone acts as a legal proxy for another. The multitude becomes a people when every individual contracts with every other individual to make the same person (either an individual or a meeting) their legal representative: 'A Multitude of men, are made *One* Person, when they are by one man, or one Person, represented ... Every man giving their common Representer, Authority from himself in particular; and owning all the actions the Representer doth.'[17]

For Hobbes, therefore, the multitude exists in three distinct moments: before the contract, when there is a multitude and no people; in the contract, where the multitude becomes a people insofar as it decides to whom sovereignty should be given; and after the contract, when a proxy has been designated, and the designated proxy is now the people, and multitude itself just a multitude once more. Multitude and people only exist alongside each other during one of these moments. Prior to the formation of a commonwealth the people does not exist; later, in the contract, insofar as the multitude is the people, the multitude does not exist (and vice versa); only after the multitude, as the people, has transferred sovereign power, does it once again lapse into being 'a disorganized multitude', while the people is now the individual or collective proxy to whom that power has been transferred.[18] Thus,

> in every commonwealth the *People* Reigns; for even in *Monarchies* the *People* exercises power; for the *people* wills through the will of *one man*. But the citizens, i.e. the subjects are a *multitude*. In a *Democracy* and in an *Aristocracy* the citizens are a *multitude*, but the *council* is the *people*; in a *Monarchy* the subjects are a *multitude*, and (paradoxically) the King is the *people*.[19]

However, were it to be the case that the multitude did not designate a proxy, and everyone became a member of a democratic council, then the multitude would continue to be the people *qua* sovereign body and a multitude *qua* subjects.

It is wrong to claim that Hobbes's multitude shuns political unity, resists authority, or does not enter into lasting agreements. According to Hobbes, it is the multitude who enter into lasting agreements (with one another as individuals) to create the people. The multitude cannot be 'that which does not make itself fit to become people', for it may itself become the people. Hobbes is not opposed to the multitude, but the simulacrum of the people represented by the faction, a multitude that thinks it is a people when it is not:

> By FACTION I mean a multitude of citizens, united either by agreements with each other or by the power of one man, without authority from the holder or holders of sovereign power. A *faction* is like a commonwealth within the commonwealth; for just as a commonwealth comes into being by men's union in a natural state, so a faction comes into being by a new union of citizens.[20]

The parallels are too close for comfort. A people and a faction are formed in precisely the same way: the only difference between them is that whereas the former is comprised of the multitude in the state of nature, the latter is comprised of the multitude as citizens. There is nothing to distinguish a faction from a people save that the people already exists, and in a democracy, the existence of a people, as opposed to a multitude, continues 'only so long as a certain time and place is publicly known and appointed, on which those who so wish may convene'.[21] No wonder, as Hobbes had complained in the *Elements*, that groups of like-minded persons are prone to 'calling by the name of people any multitude of his own faction'.[22]

Res publica res populi

Although it would be impossible to learn this from the work of Negri, Balibar, Montag or Virno, Hobbes's distinction between the people and the multitude was far from original. In Cicero's dialogue, *The Republic*, Scipio defines a commonwealth as 'the property of a people' [*res publica res populi*]. But, he continues, 'a people is not any collection of human beings, but an assemblage of people in large numbers [*coetus multitudinis*] associated in an agreement with respect to justice and a partnership for the common good'.[23] This definition was picked up by Augustine in book 19 of the *City of God*: 'A people he defined as a numerous gathering united in fellowship by a common sense of right and a community of interest.'[24]

Had the Roman state ever actually met these criteria? In Cicero's definition the gathered multitude had to have two things to qualify as a people: *consensus iuris*, agreement about the law, and *communio utilitatis*, common interest. Augustine focused on the first of these. A *consensus iuris* ought to mean that all received their due, but if the true God did not receive his due, there was no justice, and if there was no justice there was no people, and 'if no people, then no people's estate, but a nondescript mob [*qualiscumque multitudinis*] unworthy of the name of people'. By its own definition, the Roman state had never existed: there was no Roman people, just a rabble. Empire and multitude were identical; the *populus Dei* was the only true people.

Having made his point, Augustine then provides a less exacting account of the distinction between a people and a multitude: 'A people is a large gathering [*coetus multitudinis*] of rational beings united in fellowship by their agreement about the objects of their love.'[25] Unworthy as the objects of its veneration had been, perhaps the Roman people had existed after all. Elsewhere, Augustine offers a still more elastic definition: 'Grant a point of unity, and a *populus* exists; take that unity away, and it is a mob [*turba*]. For what is a mob except a confused multitude [*multitudo turbata*]?'[26]

The *populus/multitudo* distinction and the role of *ius* and *utilitas* in constituting a *populus* were frequently discussed in medieval political theory, particularly after Aristotle's *Politics* was translated in the thirteenth century.[27] In book three, Aristotle had distinguished between the various forms of good and bad government in terms of whether they served the common interest or their own private advantage. So, 'when the multitude govern the state with a view to the common advantage', that government qualified as a 'polity', or, as the commentary by Thomas Aquinas and Peter of Auvergne put it, *respublica*, as opposed to merely being a democracy governing in the interests of the mob.[28]

Although it was not directly juxtaposed with Cicero's or Augustine's definitions of the state, Aristotle's *Politics* served to shift the emphasis from *ius* to *utilitas*, and from the distinction between the one and the many to that between the many and the few. From the latter perspective, the political potential of the multitude looked more promising. Aristotle had suggested that there were some respects in which the rule of the multitude was preferable to that of the few, and Marsilius of Padua pressed home the point that 'the common utility of a law is better known by the entire multitude'.[29] No one appears to have asked whether the unity needed for *consensus iuris* was equally essential for *communio utilitatis*, but the terms of the debate had changed in such a way that the question could be raised.

Unity

What is the essence of the state? When is a multitude a people and when is it not? These are questions in the alchemy of the political, and in the tradition derived from Cicero and Augustine, the answer is always unity. Multitude and people are mutually exclusive terms only because they represent different potentialities within the constitutional history of the same aggregation of persons. If there is unity, there is no plurality; if there is plurality, no unity.

For Spinoza, there is never a choice between people and multitude. He does not use the vocabulary of the *populus/multitudo* distinction in either the *Tractatus Theologico-Politicus* or the *Tractatus Politicus*. But the opposition between plurality and unity is common to both, and in both cases, Spinoza insists upon the necessity of unity for the formation and maintenance of the state. In the *Tractatus Theologico-Politicus* Spinoza describes a social contract of the Hobbesian type in which 'each individual hands over the whole of his power to the body politic', which then possesses 'sovereign natural right over all things'.[30] In the *Tractatus Politicus*, however, there is no transfer, and the multitude retains its natural right. In place of the transfer to a single sovereign body, 'the right of the commonwealth is determined by the power of the multitude, which is led, as it were, by one mind'.[31] It is through this unanimity that the multitude achieves *consensus iuris*: 'when men have *iura communia*, and all are guided as if by one mind'.[32]

It might be argued that even though the multitude is of one mind, it is still a multitude and so the right of the commonwealth is determined by the aggregated right of multiple individuals rather than by their unity. But Spinoza is at pains to emphasize that there is a distinction between men acting together as individuals, in which case their collective right is the sum of their individual right, and men coming together as one, in which case they have more than the sum of their individual right, for 'if two come together and unite their strength, they have jointly more power, and consequently more right over nature than both of them separately'.[33] Similarly, so long as men are in the state of nature, their natural right is merely hypothetical, and it is only when united, as if of one mind, that men provide for one another the collective physical security that allows them to possess natural right as individuals: 'And if this is why the schoolmen want to call man a sociable animal – I mean because men in the state of nature can hardly be independent – I have nothing to say against them.'[34]

The tradition to which Spinoza refers derives from Aristotle, who maintained that:

> The state is by nature clearly prior to the family and to the individual, since the whole is of necessity prior to the part ... The proof that the state is a creation of nature and prior to the individual is that the individual, when isolated, is not self-sufficing; and therefore he is like a part in relation to the whole.[35]

Spinoza also emphasizes the priority of the whole to the part when making a distinction between a multiplicity of individuals acting as individuals, and the multitude acting as if of one mind. Although he refers to the former as individuals and the latter as the multitude (rather than, as Hobbes had done, the former as the multitude, and the latter as the people) the substance of the distinction is the same: 'The right of the supreme authorities is nothing less than simple natural right, limited, indeed, by the power, not of every individual, but of the multitude, which is guided, as it were, by one mind.'[36]

In other words, it is not the sum of individual natural right that limits (and, by implication, constitutes) the right of the commonwealth. It is the multitude *qua* unit, not the multitude *qua* individuals, that constitutes and limits that right. The point is made in similar terms in microcosm when Spinoza later describes the functioning of an aristocracy where sovereignty resides with a council of patricians:

> Supreme authority of this dominion rests with this council as a whole, not with every individual member of it (for otherwise it would be but the gathering of an undisciplined mob [*nam alias coetus esset inordinatae multitudinis*]). It is, therefore, necessary that all the patricians be so bound by the laws as to form, as it were, one body governed by one mind.[37]

The '*coetus multitudinis*' is not, for Spinoza, any more than it is for Cicero or Augustine, the bearer of right, unless it is united: '*una veluti mente*'.

Rather than maintaining that 'the multitude is a multiplicity' or 'a plurality which persists as such', Spinoza only ascribes a positive political role to it when it is one, i.e., when it is a people in all but name. He does not attribute the right of the commonwealth to the power of the multitude as a plurality of individual wills, but to the power of the multitude 'led as it were by one mind'. And the right of the commonwealth diminishes in direct proportion to the degree that such unity is not maintained. Without unity the multitude would barely even possess right individually, but without multiplicity nothing would be lost, for multiplicity signifies weakness rather than strength, an incapacity to act rather than the power of acting.

For Hobbes, the essential characteristic of the multitude is always its plurality, in that when it is unified and sovereign it ceases to be a multitude and becomes a people. According to Spinoza, a multitude is always a multitude, even when it is united and sovereign. But the fact that he does not make the verbal distinction does not mean that he denies to the multitude those qualities that Hobbes thinks make it a people. For Spinoza, had he used these terms, the people is a moment of the multitude, a moment he wants to last forever.

Reason

The primary difference between Hobbes and Spinoza is to be found not in their divergent approach to the question of plurality and unity in relation to sovereignty, but rather in their account of the conditions that make unity possible. Spinoza repeatedly insists that the multitude can be one only if guided by reason:

> For the right of the commonwealth is determined by the power of the multitude, which is led, as it were, by one mind. But this unity of mind can in no wise be conceived, unless the commonwealth pursues chiefly the very end, which sound reason teaches is to the interest [*utile*] of all men.[38]

Sovereignty is impossible without unity, and unity is impossible without reason, for 'it is impossible for a multitude to be guided, as it were, by one mind, as under dominion is required, unless it has laws ordained according to the dictate of reason'.[39]

Spinoza here continues to follow the logic of the part and the whole. As he explained in a letter of 1665, 'On the question of whole and parts, I consider things as parts of a whole to the extent that their natures adapt themselves to one another so that they are in the closest possible agreement.'[40] Applied to humanity this carried the implication that men are parts of a social whole only to the extent that they follow reason, for as he explained in the *Ethics*, 'insofar as men are subject to passions, they cannot be said to agree in nature', and 'only insofar as men live according to the guidance of reason, must they always agree in nature'.[41]

But there is an apparently insuperable problem here, for 'such as persuade themselves that the multitude ... can ever be induced to live according to the bare dictate of reason must be dreaming of the poetic golden age or of a stage play'.[42] Indeed, as Spinoza had complained in the *Tractatus Theologico-Politicus*, 'the fickle disposition of the multitude almost reduces those who have experience of it to despair, for it is governed solely by emotions, not by reason'.[43] And in fact it is not even reason that impels men to seek society, for 'a multitude comes together, and wishes to be guided, as it were, by one mind, not at the suggestion of reason but of some common passion' – hope, fear or vengeance.[44]

So how is it possible for the 'fickle multitude', who are governed by emotions, to be united by reason? The problem had already been discussed by Aristotle and his medieval commentators. As Peter of Auvergne emphasized, the multitude has a double aspect. On the one hand, there is a bestial multitude in which no one has reason; on the other, a multitude where all have some share in reason and are therefore also amenable to rational persuasion. In the former case, the multitude is unfit to rule, but in the latter, the rule of the multitude is actually better than that of a few wise individuals.[45]

Aristotle had explained that as the multitude coheres, individual emotions cancel one another out, and reasonable judgements prevail. Whereas 'the individual is liable to be overcome by anger or by some other passion ... it is hardly to be supposed that a great number of persons would all get into a passion and go wrong at the same moment'. So 'although individually they may be worse judges than those who have special knowledge – as a body they are as good or better'.[46] According to Aristotle, this is the chief argument in favour of the view that 'the multitude ought to be supreme rather than the few ... for the many, of whom each individual is but an ordinary person, when they meet together may very likely be better than the few good, if regarded not individually but collectively ... For each individual among the many has a share of virtue and prudence, and when they meet together they become in a manner one man, who has many feet, and hands and senses; that is a figure of their mind and disposition.'[47]

Spinoza rehearses this argument in the *Tractatus Theologico-Politicus*, where he suggests that in a democracy, irrational commands are less to be feared than in other forms of government because 'it is almost impossible that the majority of a people, especially if it be a large one, should agree in an irrational design'. Indeed, Spinoza sees this principle as being intrinsic to the nature of democracy, for 'the basis and aim of a democracy is to avoid the desires as irrational, and to bring men as far as possible under the control of reason'.[48]

In the *Tractatus Politicus*, this is the rationale for the expansion of the numbers on a council; for 'the dominion conferred upon a large enough council is absolute, or approaches nearest to the absolute. For if there be an absolute dominion, it is, in fact, that which is held by an entire multitude.'[49] Spinoza's argument for the expansion of the decision-making process to accommodate the entire irrational multitude is a function, not of his respect for the judgement of the individuals who comprise the multitude, but of the belief that as the numbers involved increase, so too will the reliance on reason and thus the possibility of unity.

> While a few are deciding everything in conformity with their own passions only, liberty and the general good are lost. For men's natural abilities are too dull to see through everything at once; but by consulting, listening, and debating, they grow more acute, and while they are trying all means, they at last discover those which they want, which all approve, but no one would have thought of in the first place.[50]

The multitude are of one mind, not through affective imitation, but only insofar as they are guided by reason. And it is through their aggregation that reason prevails.

Utility

According to Hobbes, there are some societies that do 'govern themselves in multitude' and cohere without a contract in the way that Spinoza implies,[51] but they are animal societies, not human ones.

> Among the animals which Aristotle calls political he counts not only *Man* but many others too, including the *Ant*, the *Bee*, etc. For although they are devoid of reason, which would enable them to make agreements and submit to government, still by their consenting, i.e. by desiring and avoiding the same objects, they so direct their actions to a common end that their swarms are not disturbed by sedition. Yet their swarms are still not *commonwealths*, and so the animals themselves should not be called *political*; for their government is only an accord, or many wills with one object, not (as a commonwealth needs) one will.[52]

In Hobbes's view, bees and ants achieve concord by 'desiring and avoiding the same objects', rather like the ancient Romans who, in Augustine's account, achieved a form of statehood by virtue of prizing the same things. What social animals lack is unity of the will.

> An *accord* between several parties, i.e. an association formed only for mutual aid, does not afford to the parties ... the *laws of nature* ... (An *accord* of several persons ... consists only in their all directing their actions to the same end and to a *common good*.) But something more is needed, an element of fear, to prevent an accord on

peace and mutual assistance for a *common good* from collapsing in
discord when a *private good* subsequently comes into conflict with
the *common good*.[53]

Here, Hobbes argues that *communio utilitatis* is not enough
either. Even if the multitude is working together for the
common good, they still need *consensus iuris*, in order to
resolve the disputes that inevitably arise when private
advantage does not coincide with the public good. Ants and
bees differ from human beings in this respect, for 'amongst
these creatures the Common good differeth not from the
Private; and being by nature enclined to their private, they
procure thereby the common benefit'.[54]

For Hobbes, it is only the absence of reason that allows
public and private goods to coincide, for unlike rational
beings, social animals are not given to comparing themselves with others, and arguing about what is really in the
common interest. In contrast, Spinoza argues that men are
incapable of agreement just insofar as they are governed
by passions, and that it is through reason that private and
public goods coincide. His thinking on this point emerges
most clearly in the *Ethics*, where he states that 'since reason demands nothing contrary to Nature, it demands that
everyone love himself, seek his own advantage', and that it
is 'when each man most seeks his own advantage for himself
… [that] … men are most useful to one another'.[55] It is in
this regard that man is truly a social animal and achieves the
unity, as if of one mind, to which Spinoza repeatedly refers
in the *Tractatus Politicus*:

> Man, I say, can wish for nothing more helpful to the preservation
> of his being than that all should so agree in all things that the minds
> and bodies of all would compose, as it were, one mind [*unam quasi*
> *mentem*] and one body; that all should strive together, as far as they
> can, to preserve their being; and that all, together, should seek for
> themselves the common advantage [*commune utile*] of all.[56]

To Hobbes's 'man is wolf to man', Spinoza responds 'man is
god to man' – but only because, like the wolf, he is a 'social
animal'.

The paradox is a reminder that insofar as Spinoza's political philosophy differs from that of Hobbes, it is due to his
reworking of three Aristotelian themes: man is a social animal, always part of a whole; the many are more rational than
the few; the state is a union for common benefit. Whereas
Aristotle made no connection between these points, Spinoza
starts to thread them together. Because man is a social animal, people seek association; through association they gain
access to a rationality they would not possess as individuals
or in smaller groups; this rationality is the source of common
utility, for 'insofar as men live according to the guidance
of reason, they must do only those things that are good for
human nature, and hence, for each man'.[57] The passions foster sociability; sociability rationality, and rationality utility.
And so it is necessarily the case that as the commonwealth
approaches the rule of the multitude (who, by virtue of their
numbers, are more likely to embody reason), the private
good approximates more closely to the public.

Nowhere in this sequence is there any mention of a contract, or need to mention one. Although Spinoza insists

on unity in both the *Tractatus Theologico-Politicus* and the *Tractatus Politicus*, somewhere between the two he must have realized that the account of reason given in the *Ethics* made the contract superfluous, for the multitude could be of one mind without having decided to be so. Unintentionally, Spinoza had opened the way for accounts of the state that dispensed not only with the contract but with the intersubjective unity of reason as well.

The invisible hand

Such accounts were not long in coming. Mandeville's claim that 'The worst of all the Multitude / Did something for the Common Good' is, it is now apparent, doubly provocative. That the worst members of society should be making a contribution to its welfare is obviously surprising, but even the claim that the multitude *qua* multitude act for the common good undermines the long tradition in which it was, by definition, the people not the multitude who promote the common good.

However, Mandeville has his own paradoxical version of the people/multitude distinction:

I hope that the reader knows that by society I understand a body politic, in which man ... is become a disciplined creature that can find his own ends in labouring for others, and where under one head or other form of government each member is rendered subservient to the whole, and all of them by cunning management are made to act as one. For if by society we only mean a number of people, that without rule or government should keep together out of a natural affection to their species or love of company, such as a herd of cows

or a flock of sheep, then there is not in the world a more unfit creature for society than man.[58]

The implied distinction is between those animals that are
truly political, and those that are merely aggregated. But
Mandeville does not suppose that the former constitute a
body politic because they have made a contract with one
another. Instead, he ridicules the idea that 'two or three
hundred single savages ... could ever establish a society,
and be united into one body'. Society as a whole developed from pre-existing forms of sociability, which were
the product not of 'the good and amiable, but the bad and
hateful qualities of man'.[59]

Mandeville's point is that sociability is in fact an emergent
property of individualism, the body politic an unforeseen
consequence of vice. Humankind could not remain a lead-
erless flock even if it wanted to. But in place of Spinoza's
reason, he substitutes pride as the instrument through which
individual desires converge for the common interest. There
is 'no other quality so beneficial', for with men, 'the more
their pride and vanity are displayed ... the more capable
they must be of being raised into large and vastly numerous
societies'.[60] The worst of all the multitude do not just do
something for the common good, they do the most.

Mandeville's favourite example is the way in which the
ostentation of the few provides employment for the many,
and in *The Theory of Moral Sentiments*, Adam Smith restates
Mandeville's argument: despite their 'natural selfishness and
rapacity', the rich, whose sole end is 'the gratification of
their own vain and insatiable desires', employ the labour

of thousands, and are led 'by an invisible hand to … without intending it, without knowing it, advance the interest of society'.[61] Not just the imprudent rich, but, in *The Wealth of Nations*, other economic actors, too, like the merchant who prefers domestic to foreign investment, are 'in this, as in many other cases, led by an invisible hand to promote an end which was no part of his intention'.[62]

Smith himself does not seem to have attached much significance to the term, but others realized that the 'invisible hand' potentially offered an explanation not only for the economic order of society, but the political as well:

The governments which the world has hitherto seen, have seldom or never taken their rise from deep-laid schemes of human policy. In every state of society which has yet existed, the multitude has, in general, acted from the immediate impulse of passion, or from the pressure of their wants and necessities; and, therefore, what we commonly call the political order, is, at least in a great measure, the result of the passions and wants of man, combined with the circumstances of his situation; or, in other words, it is chiefly the result of the wisdom of nature. So beautifully, indeed, do these passions and circumstances act in subservience to her designs, and so invariably have they been found, in the history of past ages, to conduct him in time to certain beneficial arrangements, that we can hardly bring ourselves to believe that the end was not foreseen by those engaged in the pursuit. Even in those rude periods, when, like the lower animals, he follows blindly his instinctive principles of action, he is led by an invisible hand, and contributes his share to the execution of a plan, of the nature and advantages of which he has no conception. The operations of the bee, when it begins, for the first time, to form its cell, convey to us a striking image of the efforts of unenlightened Man, in conducting the operations of an infant government.[63]

Hayek? No, Dugald Stewart, Smith's pupil and biographer, and the first to acknowledge Smith's dependence on Mandeville. Here, Rousseau's question about the 'blind multitude' receives its answer – an answer with which Spinoza could not have disagreed.

General intellect versus general will

For those, like Rousseau, who think that even though private and public interests sometimes coincide, there can be no enduring harmony between the two, some sort of distinction between the will of all (represented by the sum of private interests) and the general will (that is in the common interest) will always be necessary.[64] But for those who can see the workings of an invisible hand, this dichotomy represents a 'false alternative between the rule of one and chaos'.[65] Rousseau may consider the will of all to be 'an incoherent cacophony', but as 'the plural expression of the entire population' it is, Hardt and Negri suggest, more like 'an orchestra with no conductor – an orchestra that through constant communication determines its own beat and would be thrown off and silenced only by the imposition of a conductor's central authority'.[66]

Like that of their predecessors, Hardt and Negri's model of 'the collective intelligence that can emerge from the communication and co-operation of a varied multiplicity' comes from the natural world. Taking up 'the notion of the swarm from the collective behaviour of social animals, such as ants, bees, and termites, to investigate multi-agent-distributed systems of intelligence', they focus on the multitude's 'swarm intelligence'; its ability to make 'swarm music' without a conductor or a centre that dictates order.[67] On this account,

> just as the multitude produces in common, just as it produces the common, it can produce political decisions ... What the multitude produces is not just goods and services; the multitude also and most importantly produces co-operation, communication, forms of life, and social relationships. The economic production of the multitude, in other words, is not only a *model* for political decision-making but also tends itself to *become* political decision-making.[68]

In the work of Virno, this common production is expressed in the opposition between the general will and the general intellect: 'The One of the multitude, then, is not the One of the people. The multitude does not converge into a *volonté générale* for one simple reason: because it already has access to a *general intellect*.'[69] Developed from Marx's passing reference to the moment when 'general social knowledge has become a *direct force of production*',[70] the general intellect is presented as 'the know-how on which social productivity relies ... [This does] not necessarily mean the aggregate of knowledge acquired by the species, but the *faculty* of thinking; potential as such, not its countless particular realizations.'[71]

If this sounds suspiciously like 'tacit knowledge' as it appears in the writings of Michael Polanyi and Hayek, the affinity is unsurprising, for multitude itself is what they would have termed 'a polycentric order' within which 'actions are determined by the relation and mutual adjustment to each other of the elements of which it consists'.[72] For Hardt and Negri too, the model for such an order is the brain, where 'there is no one that makes a decision ... but rather a swarm, a multitude that acts in concert'.[73] In both cases, the resulting patterns are the accumulated problem-solving techniques of the species, 'our habits and skills, our emotional attitudes, our tools, and our institutions', or, as Virno puts it, our 'imagination, ethical propensities, mind-sets, and "linguistic games"'.[74] For Hardt and Negri, 'habit is the common in practice: the common that we continually produce and the common that serves as the basis of our actions'.[75]

If the multitude is a polycentric order, swarm intelligence an invisible hand, and the general intellect a form of tacit knowledge, these are not coincidental affinities (or products of a wholesale borrowing from Hayek) but the direct result of Negri's adherence to those aspects of Spinoza's thought that lead away from Hobbes. From Cicero onwards, it was axiomatic that only when unified into a people could a multitude become a political agent. Spinoza does not fundamentally dissent, but he nevertheless draws together a variety of Aristotelian themes to articulate an interpretation of unity that does not depend on the conscious agreement of all involved. Insofar as Spinoza differs from Hobbes, his thought leads to Mandeville, Smith, Stewart and Hayek.

The multitude is not a new political agent invented by Spinoza, or the losing side in the political struggles of the seventeenth century; it was always the raw material of the political. The only question was: how could the multitude become an agent? Only two answers are offered by the tradition of which Spinoza forms a part, and within which his thought is a watershed: either the multitude is united and acts as a single agent, or the multitude remains disparate and uncoordinated, but nevertheless acts collectively through the working of an invisible hand.

Contemporary champions of the multitude remain trapped within this history, committed to a position that is ultimately either Hobbesian or Hayekian. Seeking a route out of the impasse posed by the global market and its reactive populisms, they have retraced the path that led to it. The difficulty comes from starting with the multitude as an aggregation of individuals, and then proceeding to dichotomize the one and the many. Agency is then transformed into a choice between general will or general intellect, state or society. Rather than being an agent of limitless potential, the multitude contracts political possibility to the primitivisms of the security state and the free market. Within contemporary politics, the problem of agency demands a more complex resolution.

4
States of Failure

The state is not 'abolished': it withers away.

Engels, *Anti-Dühring*

The more the social bond is stretched the slacker it becomes.

Rousseau, *The Social Contract*

The previous chapter argued that the contemporary crisis of political agency reflects the division between the aggregated outcomes of individual choice and the decisions of the collective will. Yet the contraction of political possibility to the invisible hand of the market and populist reaction does not restrict individual actors to one or the other. It is precisely because different types of agency are not exclusive to particular actors that the cycle of unintended effect and ineffectual intent is so obvious. Appealing to the agency of the multitude serves only to reinforce the divide, for the multitude acts either as one or as many, and becomes a political agent either through the unity of the will or through the workings of the invisible hand. Starting with the multitude, as early modern political theory invariably did (and as Negri, Hardt and Virno now propose to do once more), results in a dichotomy: general will or general intellect, the political or the social, state or society.

To these divisions, the Hegelian theory of the state offers a resolution. Hegel consciously worked with a double inheritance: on one hand, a conception of the state as the united will of the multitude, on the other, an account of civil society in which society is governed not by the will, but by the rationality of the invisible hand. Though versions of the former were at least as old as Cicero, Hegel gave Rousseau the credit 'for adducing the will as the principle of the state'. However, he complained (somewhat unfairly) that Rousseau 'takes the will only in a determinate form as the individual will, and he regards the rational will not as the absolutely rational element in the will, but only as a "general" will which proceeds out of this individual will as out of a conscious will'. Rousseau had undermined 'the divine principle of the state' by reducing 'the union of individuals in the state to a contract and therefore to something based on their arbitrary wills'. The consequences could be seen in the French Revolution, which embodied only the arbitrary will and not the rational, and so ended in the 'maximum of frightfulness and terror'.[1]

Hegel's vision of civil society, and the role of the invisible hand of the market within it, is derived from Ferguson and Smith and feeds into Marx's idea of the social.[2] In the course of achieving selfish ends, 'there is formed a system of complete interdependence, wherein the livelihood, happiness, and legal status of one man is interwoven with the livelihood, happiness, and rights of all'.[3] Although 'each individual is his own end, and all else means nothing to him … he cannot accomplish the full extent of his ends without reference to others'. And so 'through its reference to others, the particular end takes on the form of universality, and gains satisfaction by simultaneously satisfying the welfare of others'.[4] However, for Hegel, civil society too has its limitations. Because its rationality relies upon the mechanism of the invisible hand, particularity (the individual agent) and universality (the product of the invisible hand) remain disjoined: 'Unity is present here not as freedom but as necessity, since it is by compulsion that the particular rises to the form of universality.'[5]

In Hegel's account, the limitation inherent in the rationality of the invisible hand is its unintended, unwilled emergence, while the problem with the unity of the will is its arbitrary nature and potentially destructive consequences. Both are overcome in the fusion of the two in the state. According to Hegel, it is through the invisible hand that individuals become aware of their own unity. When men are interdependent and 'reciprocally related to one another in their work and the satisfaction of their needs, subjective self-seeking turns into a contribution to the satisfaction of the needs of everyone else'. In this way, 'self-seeking turns into the mediation of the particular through the universal'.[6] Thanks to the invisible hand, 'if I further my ends, I further the ends of the universal, and this in turn furthers my end'.[7]

Because 'a particular end … is attained in the simultaneous attainment of the welfare of others', it follows that 'individuals can attain their ends only in so far as they themselves determine their knowing, willing, and acting in a universal way'.[8] So when, through the invisible hand, particular self-consciousness is raised to consciousness of its universality, its knowing and willing becomes 'formal freedom and formal universality' insofar as its universality is no longer that of necessity but of a will conscious of its universality:

> Particular interests not only achieve their complete development and gain explicit recognition for their right ... they also pass over of their own accord into the interest of the universal ... they know and will the universal; they even recognize it as their own substantive mind; they take it as their end and aim and are active in its pursuit ... In the very act of willing these [their own private ends] they will the universal in the light of the universal.[9]

In practice, this involves the 'consciousness that my interest, both substantive and particular, is contained and preserved in another's (i.e. in the state's) interest and end'.[10] This is the essence of patriotism, but it is also simultaneously the ground of the rationality of the state, for 'the state is absolutely rational inasmuch as it is the actuality of the substantial will which it possesses in the particular self-consciousness once that consciousness has been raised to consciousness of its universality'.[11]

Hegel's theory of the state acknowledges that there is frequently a disjunction between the aggregated outcomes of our individual actions, and the objectives for which we collectively strive. He describes the collective product of civil society, brought about through 'the complex interdependence of each on all' as a sort of general intellect which 'presents itself to each as the universal permanent capital which gives each the opportunity, by the exercise of his education and skill, to draw a share from it'.[12] However, he is clear that this is not the same as the general will, as expressed in a social contract. So, instead of wills being united by their own volition, the invisible hand creates a unity which is then consciously willed. In effect, the state is the 'general intellect' become conscious of itself as the general will. By this means, the arbitrariness of the general will is steadied by the rationality of the invisible hand, and the spontaneous order of society is infused with the patriotism of the state.

Spinoza had opened up the possibility that there might be a source of political unity distinct from that of the will. Hegel, aware that this potentially creates a problem of agency in complex societies, brings them back together again. In so doing, he offers the first theory of the modern state. Hegel's state is, as Bosanquet described it, 'society armed with force', the invisible hand clenched into an iron fist.

Shopping and bombing

If the significance of Hegel's theory of the state now appears largely forgotten, it is the result of the concerted campaign against it in the first half of the twentieth century. In 1917, L. T. Hobhouse, reading Hegel in his Highgate garden, was interrupted by the sounds of a German bombing raid. Picking up his book again, he realized that he had 'just witnessed the visible and tangible outcome of a false and wicked doctrine, the foundations of which lay, as I believe, in the book before me ... the Hegelian theory of the god-state'.[13]

In fact, Hobhouse was responding not so much to Hegel himself as to Bosanquet, whose *Philosophical Theory of the State* recast the Hegelian theory in terms derived from only one of Hegel's sources, Rousseau. Insensible to the workings of the invisible hand, but conscious that Hegel had neglected Rousseau's distinction between the 'general will' and the 'will of all', Bosanquet offered an account of the state in which the 'real will' embodies rationality and so becomes the will for the common good, while the will of all remains the sum of private impulses and interests. So, in Bosanquet's perhaps unfortunate analogy, the 'will of all' is like the seemingly united action of a crowd streaming away from a military parade in search of refreshment, while the 'real will' is embodied by the precision of the army whose 'every unit moves with reference to the movements of a great whole'.[14]

Hobhouse protested that if 'our real will is the general will, and the general will is most fully embodied in the state', the result is total subservience to the government. Although an action may be both general and willed, it does not follow that there is any corresponding agent, in the form of a general will:

> The life of society is not the product of coherent thinking by a single mind. On the contrary, many customs and institutions, which make up social life, have grown up in a detached, sporadic, unconscious, often unreasonable fashion.[15]

Even the rule of law is a process created from 'innumerable conflicts of innumerable wills ... contrasting very clearly with the simple and crisp decisions of an individual mind'.[16]

In this exchange, the terms of the liberal critique of the state were established, later to be echoed by others for whom the embodiment of the Hegelian state was not Wilhelmine Germany but the Third Reich and the Soviet Union. But if the liberal rejection of the Hegelian theory of political agency sought to emphasize spontaneous order at the expense of the unified will, the conservative response to Hegel has been to try to preserve the integrity of the state from the contamination of civil society.[17]

According to Carl Schmitt, Hegel's legacy had been appropriated by liberalism, but the day Hitler came to power was the day the liberal Hegel died. Although the distinction had subsequently lost its clarity, Hegel had shown that 'the state is qualitatively distinct from society and higher than it'. The state presupposed not society, but 'the political', and since the 'political' is the capacity to decide between friend and enemy, the state is not an expression of society but 'an organized political entity that decides for itself the friend-enemy distinction'. As such it is inextricably linked to the ability to wage war, for 'the friend, enemy, and combat concepts receive their real meaning precisely because they refer to the real possibility of physical killing'.[18]

By providing an alternative ancestry for the state, Schmitt tried to cut away the ground from those who (quite correctly) invoked the positive role of civil society in the Hegelian theory. For Schmitt, the state was eroded by any confusion between the two: 'The equation state = politics becomes erroneous and deceptive the moment when state and society penetrate each other.' When this is allowed to happen, 'the state turns into society ... A politically united people becomes, on the one hand, a culturally interested public, and, on the other, partially an industrial concern and its employers, partially a mass of consumers.' Whereas political unity is founded on decisions about life and death, civil society only generates consumer interest groups – 'customers purchasing gas from the same utility company, or passengers travelling on the same bus'.[19]

Associated, on the one hand, with the expansionist ambitions of the Second and Third Reichs, and, on the other, with the failings of the Weimar Republic, the Hegelian theory of the state never recovered. The double assault continues in the neo-liberal attack on the state and the neo-conservative attack on society, and is reflected in the polarization of the political and the social into the competing claims of either the general will or the general intellect – a dichotomy that is the direct result of the repudiation of the Hegelian attempt to work with both/and. This limits our ability to get a conceptual grasp of problems of agency, for separating the actions of the will from the workings of the invisible hand means that there is no framework within which to articulate problems derived from the complex interaction of both.

The enduring value of Hegel's theory lies not, as its earlier proponents and critics both imagined, in its articulation of the totalizing power of the state, but in its innovative attempt to describe the state as a solution to the problems of political agency generated by social complexity. From this perspective, the contemporary crisis has a brutal clarity.

The cycle of unintended effect and ineffectual intent is a coordination problem: a repeated failure fully to align the will with the workings of the invisible hand. There are clusters of shoppers unable to will the aggregated outcome of their own actions; and communities of bombers unable to acknowledge the arbitrariness of their own will. The fact that the same human agents are involved in both makes no difference. Instead of willing the rationality of the global market, the will is impeding its operation through reactive nationalisms. Improved coordination would instead infuse the global market with the will to violent enforcement and create a global market state. Or as Hegel's critics might put it, target the bombing in alignment with the world's shopping.

Put in these terms, the curious misalignments of contemporary global political agency become more explicable, and the limitations of their theoretical alternatives more apparent. If the logic of political agency can only be fully realized in a global market state, those wedded to the cosmopolitan idea of creating a global civil society short of a state are ignoring the decisive role of the will; but the prospect of a global state that ignores the invisible hand is equally unrealistic, for anyone who relies solely on the will is condemned to the unintended consequences of their own irrationality.

Is there then no alternative to the global market state which also allows for the agency of both the will and the invisible hand? Hegel does not describe one, but his account allows us to locate a route and a mechanism through which that alternative might be found, and to find the theoretical resources through which it might be articulated. It can be neither the general will nor the general intellect alone, nor any conjunction in which the general intellect becomes the general will; it can only be a process through which, as it were, the general will is transformed into the general intellect. For Hegel, the solution to the problem of political agency was to will the default; the alternative is to default on the will.

Entropic states

For Hegel, there is no anti-dialectic, and the state is 'an absolute unmoved end in itself'.[20] But, following Aristotle, he acknowledges that there is also a sense in which it is prior, and 'reveals itself as the true ground' of the family and civil society. He offers no account of this, though it is perhaps possible to locate a precedent in the dissolution of the family and passage to civil society. In the peaceful expansion of the family lies the origin of the particularity that inevitably destroys unity. For a family inevitably becomes a plurality of families each of which 'conducts itself as a self-subsistent concrete person' and so gives rise to the particularity that seeks its own satisfaction. Such particularity potentially dissolves not only the family, but any form of the state unable to accommodate it. So in antiquity, the development of particularity appeared as 'an invasion of ethical corruption and as the ultimate cause of the world's downfall'.[21]

But can something analogous happen to a state that, unlike the states of antiquity, already to some degree unites universality and particularity? Can 'the march of God in the world' be reversed? In the Marxist tradition, at least, the answer to that question was always unambiguously but obscurely positive. As Engels famously put it:

> The state was the official representative of society as a whole, its concentration in a visible corporation. But it was this only insofar as it was the state of that class which alone in its epoch represented society as a whole … When the state finally becomes truly the representative of society as a whole, it makes itself superfluous … The government of the persons is replaced by the administration of things, and by the direction of the processes of production. The state is not 'abolished'. *It withers away.*[22]

Commenting on this passage in *The State and Revolution*, Lenin noted that the phrase 'withers away' indicated 'both the gradualness of the process and its spontaneous nature', but emphasized that this could only mean that the state would wither away after the revolution.[23] A dictatorship of the proletariat would then take the place of the bourgeois state, and it would be this state, the proletarian state, that would gradually disappear in the higher phase of communism as the free exchange of services replaced bourgeois right.

As Lenin emphasizes, the withering away of the state takes place spontaneously, through the working of something like an invisible hand. But this is not the invisible hand of the market which ensures that when each seek their own satisfaction they supply the needs of others. Within civil society an invisible hand transforms particularity into universality; in the withering away of the state it transforms universality into particularity. The former coordinates desires, the latter disperses coercion. No invisible hand is required to satisfy needs in the higher phase of a communist society, for these are met by the free exchange of services; here an invisible hand is needed to disarm the state and restore to individuals power over themselves and each other.

The logic of this process is simple. The state is 'a special coercive force', and since, as Marx had pointed out, the unity on which the Hegelian state depended represented the rationality of a particular class, the state was nothing but 'a machine for the suppression of one class by another'. When, following the revolution, the dictatorship of the proletariat has suppressed all other classes, there is only one class, and so the need for the 'special coercive force' provided by the state simply disappears. In the case of the family, expansion had undermined the unity needed to sustain it; in the case of the state, the expansion of the universal class dissolves the difference needed for the state to maintain its identity.

In the *Prison Notebooks*, Gramsci describes this process in explicitly Hegelian terms as the state's transformation into civil society:

It is possible to imagine the coercive element of the state withering away by degrees, as ever more conscious elements of regulated society (or ethical State or civil society) make their appearance … In the doctrine of the state becoming regulated society, between a phase in which 'State' will be equal to 'government', and one in which 'State' will be identified with 'civil society', we will have to pass through a phase of the night-watchman State – i.e. of a coercive organization which will safeguard the development of the

continually proliferated elements of regulated society, and which
will therefore progressively reduce its own authoritarian and forc-
ible interventions.[24]

However, Gramsci's version of the withering away of the
state no longer presupposes the revolution: the dictatorship
of the proletariat is still the night-watchman state, but this
is now expressed through the hegemony of the party, which
'has "*de facto* power", and exercises the hegemonic function
... of holding the balance between the various interests on
"civil society"'. On this basis, it may not be possible to re-
create a traditional type of state and constitutional law, but
it is possible to inculcate the will to conform and with it
the transition from coercion to consent which ensures that
'the State's goal is its own end, its own disappearance, in
other words the re-absorption of political society into civil
society'.[25] For Hegel, civil society was an economic sphere
created from the dissolution of the family; for Gramsci, it
is also the state disarmed.

Pluralism

Gramsci's dream of the reabsorption of the state into civil
society was not merely a gloss on the pronouncements of
Engels and Lenin, it was an articulation of a fantasy widely
shared in early twentieth-century Europe. To theorists of
many political orientations it appeared that the state was
an institution destined to disappear as the administrative
capacities of civil society expanded. In England, Ernest
Barker spoke of the 'discredited state', and in France
Édouard Berth proclaimed the state to be dead or dying.[26]

For Schmitt this prospect was a nightmare. The transition from state to society could not be expressed in the gentle imagery of etiolation and reabsorption; it was part massacre, part cannibal feast. The state is the mythical Leviathan, torn apart by the horns of Behemoth. As the flesh of Leviathan was devoured by the Jews, who 'eat the flesh of the slaughtered peoples and are sustained by it', so 'political parties slaughter the mighty Leviathan, and each cuts from its corpse a piece of flesh for itself'.[27] The organizations of civil society are 'used like knives ... to cut up the Leviathan and divide his flesh amongst themselves'.[28]

Schmitt's target, here bizarrely represented by the Jews, is French syndicalism and English pluralism. Syndicalist writers like Maxime Leroy imagined the transition from the government of persons to the administration of things taking place through civil contracts: 'If there is contract, public power is dissolved within the personality of civil society; if there is civil society, there is no longer obedience, nor hierarchy, but collaboration, management, commerce.'[29] In contrast, the English writer J. N. Figgis emphasized that in pluralism the state is composed, not of 'a sand-heap of individuals, all equal and undifferentiated, unrelated except to the State, but an ascending hierarchy of groups, family, school, town, country, union, Church, etc'.[30] Whereas the syndicalists thought primarily in terms of occupational groups, Figgis's model was always the church. But they too would have endorsed Figgis's claim that 'the battle of freedom in this century is the battle of small societies to maintain their inherent life as against the all-devouring Leviathan of the whole'.[31]

If that battle were won, the state would be reabsorbed by the associations of which it was composed. These are stable social entities (as Figgis emphasized, the church was not 'a fortuitous concourse of ecclesiastical atoms'), and so their identity would reflect the pre-existing make-up of civil society. In Hegel's case this would have meant the reabsorption of the state by corporations (by which he chiefly meant guilds or professions), for it was through the corporation that the invisible hand works to ensure that 'a selfish purpose, directed towards its particular self-interest, apprehends and evinces itself at the same time as the universal', and it is through them that 'the sphere of civil society passes over into the state'.[32]

In contrast, Gramsci, like Figgis, considered the church the archetype of civil society, and occupational groups only one among the host of entities that made it up. But in Gramsci's case, unlike that of the pluralists and syndicalists, the withering away of the state does not merely restore the autonomy of civil society, it also transforms it.

Serialization

For Hegel, the state was 'an organization each of whose members is itself a group … and hence no one of its moments should appear as an unorganized aggregate'.[33] But were the anti-dialectic to go through (or bypass) the corporation and return to the most basic level of civil society, it would arrive not at the state of nature, but at the Many. Without organization, Hegel saw the Many as 'nothing but a heap, an aggregate of atomic units', Figgis's 'sand-heap of individuals', all 'somewhat connected … but connected only as an aggregate, a formless mass'.[34]

It is this possibility that Sartre systemizes in hallucinatory detail in the *Critique of Dialectical Reason*. For him, too, 'the basic type of sociality' is the collective, the 'inert gathering with its structure of seriality', which he equates with Hegel's 'atomized crowd'.[35] His most famous example is the bus queue where, despite having the appearance of a social group, everyone is isolated from everyone else and linked only through their alienation, which is what constitutes them in their mutual isolation.

But unlike Schmitt, who also used the example of bus passengers, Sartre emphasizes that an inert gathering like this can be transformed in an instant, 'by the flash of a common *praxis*', when it recognizes its common interest.[36] The origin of this 'totalization', as Sartre calls it, is 'individual freedom conceived as the will of all'.[37] Individuals fleeing from a common enemy realize that 'it is neither Others, nor a few individuals, who flee: instead, flight, conceived as a common *praxis* reacting to a common threat, *becomes flight* as an active totality'. Everyone reacts in a new way: 'not as an individual, nor as an Other, but as an individual incarnation of the common person'.[38]

However, this totalization is simultaneously the beginning of detotalization, a play of dialectic and anti-dialectic in which 'groups are born of series and … end up serializing themselves in their turn'.[39] Seeking to preserve itself when there is no longer a common enemy and its spontaneous unity begins to dissolve, a group-in-fusion may take a sequence of measures designed to maintain its unity and so perpetuate its own existence. But these only constitute the route back to seriality. The actions taken at each stage to remedy dissolution are actually those that produce it, and 'the group – whose origin and end reside in an effort by the individuals who are gathered together to dissolve seriality in themselves – will, in the course of its struggle, actually reproduce alterity in itself and freeze into the inorganic'.[40] The entire process of detotalization is an example of what Sartre calls 'counterfinality', or, as others have termed it, 'the invisible backhand', in which the unintended consequence of aggregated action is a state of affairs not only unforeseen, but undesired by its agents.[41]

According to Sartre, this process can be traced in the course of the French Revolution, from the storming of the Bastille (the *praxis* of a fused group) to the Convention (the institution). But although the *Critique* may be cast as a meditation on the failure of revolution, it also provides an algorithm for the entropy of the state. Indeed, Sartre explicitly equates the process with the communist vision of 'the gradual withering-away of the State in favour of broader and broader re-groupments of other-directed serialities', acknowledging that in this context the dictatorship of the proletariat is just a 'compromise between the active, sovereign group and passive seriality'.[42] Although he rejected the Hegelian account of the formation of the state, and refused any easy equation of the group-in-fusion with it, Sartre offers another way of combining unity of the will and the invisible hand. In Hegel, an invisible hand creates the unity of the will; in Sartre it undoes it.

Dissipative structures

Gramsci's talk of reabsorption, Schmitt's febrile fantasies of associations gathering round to dismember the state, and Sartre's account of serialization are all potentially descriptions of the transition from state to society. We use these strange metaphors partly because the transition itself remains largely within the imaginary, partly because the Western tradition seems to lack an adequate vocabulary for ontological failure. The best way to coordinate them is perhaps to think of them as measures of the entropy of the state, for this allows the differences between them to be quantified more easily.

Statistical measures of entropy work off some variant of Boltzmann's elegant thought experiment which demonstrated that the relationship between order and disorder might be measured in terms of the number of different ways a given distribution could be achieved. Suppose that a box is divided into two compartments and eight particles are distributed between the two. An unequal distribution will have fewer possible arrangements (there is only one way to have all eight particles on one side, eight ways to have one particle on one side and seven in the other), whereas an equal distribution will have many more (seventy, in fact). An unequal distribution is therefore relatively speaking ordered (but improbable), while an equal distribution disordered (but probable). If the number of compartments and/or the number of particles were increased, the number of possible distributions would increase and the number of arrangements would grow still further.

The state might easily be viewed in the same terms, for it is easy to see how the traditional forms of monarchy,

aristocracy and democracy represent an increasingly probable but disordered series. So too the relationship of state and
society: the traditional state form has only one compartment;
the pluralist state has several, and the atomized heap has as
many as there are people. Putting the two together, the distribution with the highest degree of order is the monarchical
state which has only one source of power and only allows
one person to exercise it, while the maximum of disorder is a
democratic serialization in which everyone is both different
from everyone else and interchangeable with them; somewhere between the two would be an aristocratic pluralism.

Seen in these terms, the formation of the Hegelian state
represents an increasing degree of order, while its reabsorption by civil society, whether conceived in terms of some
form of pluralism or as total atomization, is an increasing
degree of disorder (more so in the latter case). However, the
progress of Hegel's dialectic is not unilinear, and an anti-
dialectic would not be either. The particularity that breaks
up the family is for Hegel also the source of the rational
unity of civil society: increasing disorder (the emergence
of particularity from the unity of the family) also produces
new forms of order (the emergent properties of the market). The invisible backhand that destroys the family and
the invisible hand that creates the market are actually one.

Translated into the language of complexity theory, this
is an example of a 'dissipative structure' – a form of order
that unexpectedly emerges as disorder increases.[43] Were
the equivalent to happen in the entropy of the state, the
resulting dissipative structures would appear as unintended
forms of social order. Whereas serialization and pluralism

imply that the state is either reduced to a heap, or else consumed by pre-existing social formations, this model opens up a third possibility between atomization and absorption. Atomization need not be simply entropic; it may also be the source of social forms generated by the process of entropy itself. In Sartre, detotalization returns the group to the point at which the dialectic can begin again; on this model, groups are formed through the process of detotalization. Or to put it another way, pluralism becomes an emergent property of serialization, and social groups (perhaps even churches) are formed through what Figgis called the 'fortuitous concourse of atoms'. What we have is nothing less than an alternative route to a fully developed civil society, in which civil society is an emergent property of increasing entropy rather than an emergent property of increasing order.

Is it necessary for that order to be the same as that of civil society prior to the formation state? No, for it is merely the mechanism that is the same, not the route, and there is no reason to assume that one set of emergent properties will be like another. In this case, it seems unlikely that the invisible hand that creates civil society and the invisible hand that recreates civil society from the remains of the state will produce similar results. Apart from anything else, they are working on different materials: one with the atomized crowd, the other with the unified state. In the former case, it is the decisions of countless individuals that produce unforeseen results, in the latter, the actions of the state itself. Even if, as Hegel argued, the state embodies the rationality of the market, the rationalization of the state will not necessarily generate the market in its place.

A Global failed state

In these hypothetical dissolutions of the Hegelian state can be discerned the proto-narratives of contemporary geopolitical analysis. Schmitt, whose early work responded to the pluralist discourse on the decline of the state, and whose later work prefigures the 'clash of civilizations', provides a bridge between the two. In *The Concept of the Political*, he argued that 'a world state which embraces the entire globe and all of humanity cannot exist ... What remains is neither politics nor state, but culture, civilization, economics, morality, law, art, entertainment, etc.'[44] Because a world state could not, by definition, be based on the political friend–enemy distinction, it would not be a state but a global civil society.

After the Second World War, Schmitt foresaw the possibility that the situation he had described might come into being. Supposing that one of the two sides in the Cold War might be victorious, there would then be 'an ultimate complete unity of the world' in which 'the victor would be the world's sole sovereign'.[45] Paradoxically, Schmitt, who had feared that Leviathan would be cut into pieces in a pluralist state, now invoked 'the great antithesis of world politics, namely the antithesis of a centrally ruled world and a balanced spatial order, of universalism and particularism, monopoly and polypoly'.[46] But whereas in the former case the state was one and civil society multiple, in the latter society is one and states are many. The alternative to the 'global spatial unity of one world order' could only be 'a plurality of *Großräume*' – spaces larger than a nation-state, each dominated by an individual hegemon.

The thesis advanced in Samuel Huntington's *Clash of Civilizations* was essentially the same. Given that a unipolar world cannot be sustained, the best way to avoid the anarchy of a global civil society is through division. Huntington therefore presents a picture of a world 'divided between a Western one and a non-Western many' moving from unipolar Western dominance to multipolarity. As the West's primacy erodes, 'much of its power will simply evaporate and the rest will be diffused on a regional basis among the several major civilizations'.[47]

Though not articulated in terms of a relationship between state and civil society, Huntington's model is conceived in terms that could be those of early twentieth-century pluralists, save that they now have a global dimension. A global state produced through the economic, military and territorial dominance of the West is now breaking up, leaving the West as one civilization among many – rather as the pluralists and syndicalists hoped the state might be reduced to one association among many. Schmitt maintained that any social conflict can become political, and in Huntington's account it is differences between civilizations that are heightened to the point at which they become conflictual.

Huntington's thesis was directed against accounts of post–Cold War politics that saw 'the universalization of Western liberal democracy as the final form of human government'. In Fukuyama's *The End of History*, for example, there are no more ideological conflicts, no more 'barbarians at the gates'. The irresistible spread of democracy, economic liberalism and technological innovation ensures that in the resulting 'universal and homogeneous state' post-historical human beings are free of all shared identities and struggle only with the vices of individualism.[48]

However, as Kojève had acknowledged, the 'universal and homogeneous state' is an oxymoron. Recognizing the homology between Schmitt's argument about a global state and the Leninist argument about the universal class, Kojève's definition of a state incorporated both. For a state to exist, it must operate with both the external distinction between friend–enemy, and an internal division between governor and governed. A state that is universal lacks the first, while one that is homogeneous lacks the second: 'The universal and homogeneous State ... is therefore neither a State nor a particular entity in general.'[49] It is, in effect, civil society in atomized form. The 'end of history' is global serialization.

The difference between the 'end of history' and the 'clash of civilizations' is therefore less fundamental than many imagine. They diverge not in the analysis itself – the shared premiss is the inevitable collapse of a global state into global civil society – but in the evaluation of the outcome: one sees global civil society as a sustainable option, the latter looks to its sub-political social divisions to regenerate a multipolar states system based not on nations but on larger civilizational blocs.

Reading analyses of the post-1989 global order in light of the early twentieth-century literature on the demise of the state reveals the former to be global variations on the themes of the latter. The convergence of these theories suggests that the master narrative of contemporary geopolitics is not, as some imagine, the move towards global sovereignty or the progress of global civil society as a step towards it. Rather it is the development of global society in place of universal coercion: the reabsorption of a global state by civil society.

The obvious contemporary focus for the process is the decline of American hegemony, still in its relatively early stages. But it is possible to see this as the final part of a longer, more complex process, a single transition of world historical importance: a global decolonization, its constituent phases so geographically various, and its political ideologies so distinct as to disguise the underlying continuity. That narrative is the decline of Western dominance from its peak in the early twentieth century. It has three distinct phases: the end of European empires, the fall of the Soviet Union and the waning of American hegemony. Each empire sought legitimacy in the demise of its predecessor, emphasizing the differences between them and concealing the extent to which all were aspects of the same thing – the three-headed monster of Western imperialism, a global state in all but name.

From such an analysis the salient features of the contemporary landscape may emerge in an unaccustomed light. Rather than being the building blocks of global politics, civilizations are perhaps the dissipative structures of the entropic global state. (As Huntington admits, 'the forces of integration in the world are real and are precisely what are generating counterforces of cultural assertion and civilizational consciousness'.) The European Union, often implicitly viewed in terms of the Hegelian dialectic as a civil society gradually creating the unity that will allow it to be willed into statehood, may also prove to be a dissipative structure of the entropy of the global state, its importance an unintended consequence of the decline of first colonial, then Soviet and now American power.

If so, its relations with the United States may become increasingly conflictual. Another corollary of this analysis is that the seemingly quixotic 'war against terror' was in fact just as central to the contemporary world as its advocates claimed. Any 'war against terror' is by definition not a war between states, but a war of the state against civil society. But this is not a war against the pre-existing structures of civil society that underlie the global state. It is a long war being fought by the global state against the dissipative structures generated by its own entropy. In which case, it may not just last forever, it may also have been going on for a lot longer than anyone suspected.

To the contemporary crisis of political agency, Hegel's theory of the state offers both an explanation (in terms of the inadequacy of any one form of agency) and two possible resolutions: it excludes the non-dialectical options of a global market society or global non-market state, and reduces the viable options to a global market state and a global, potentially non-market society. A global civil society might be willed into a global market state, or else a global state might, through the workings of the invisible hand, collapse into some form of global civil society. The former is the natural expression of the Hegelian dialectic transposed to a global context; the latter has the form of Gramsci's appropriation of the anti-dialectic.

This account relies on the workings of the invisible hand, but goes against the grain of liberal political theory. It does not start from the beginning; it insists on the need for a theory that is historically located, and it offers an account of the destruction rather than the creation of the state. Marxism acted as a corrective to liberalism in these respects, yet on this analysis, the disappearance of states founded on Marxism is an integral part of the failure of the global state. Invisible-hand explanations are usually preferred by those whom the tide of history appears to favour, while the defeated have to rely on the unity of the will. Here, the invisible hand invests the failure of utopia with the utopian promise of the failed state.

Glossing Engels, Rosa Luxemburg argued that: 'society faces a dilemma, either an advance to socialism or a reversion to barbarism'; either 'rebirth through social revolution' or else 'dissolution and decline into capitalist anarchy'.[50] The antithesis may be misleading. On this analysis, the latter may constitute the only route to the former, for the disorder of civil society is not merely statistical. In descriptions of this environment, there is a remarkable rhetorical convergence. For Hegel, it is 'a formless mass whose commotion and activity could therefore only be elementary, irrational, barbarous, and frightful'; for Sartre a 'place of violence, darkness, and witchcraft'; Luxemburg imagines it as 'shamed, dishonoured, wading in blood … a roaring beast … an orgy of anarchy'.[51]

The dissipative structures of the anti-dialectic appear as islands in this sea of disorder: oases of calm in places of violence, moments when the beast pauses for breath, periods of lassitude in the orgy.

5
Softening Up the State

Machiavelli's enduring notoriety derives from his willingness to offer political advice to anyone, and his acknowledgement that such advice may differ radically according to circumstance. The question 'What would Machiavelli say?' is rarely asked by utopian thinkers, but it is always going to be an interesting one because Machiavelli does not have a set of abstract principles from which his answers can be deduced. His analysis works only with motivations internal to the situation to which it refers, and comes without the usual side-constraints. For that reason it is always liable to surprise, redescribing the familiar in unfamiliar terms, and placing means and ends in novel relation.

To benefit from his advice, the modern reader has to reinterpret Machiavelli's historical examples and apply them to contemporary events. Machiavelli himself worked the same way, raiding both classical antiquity and Italian history for material applicable to the political crises of the sixteenth century. Recent republican interpreters have found in Machiavelli an ideal of self-government that offers an alternative to libertarian accounts of negative liberty. Meanwhile theorists on the left have focused on two diverging themes. Some, following Gramsci and Althusser and drawing primarily on *The Prince*, see Machiavelli as a prophet of unpredictable change and historical rupture, offering to all who can master fortune the possibility of making things new.[1] Others, most notably Chantal Mouffe, use the *Discourses on the First Ten Books of Livy* to argue that Machiavelli is above all the theorist of ineradicable political antagonism, whose crucial insight is that the interests of the people and the nobility are always opposed.[2]

In the latter cases, the problem that Machiavelli is being asked to address is the same: the resilience of the liberal-democratic (now neo-liberal) nation-state, which has so far proved immune to revolutionary transformation and stubbornly resistant to piecemeal reform. Is there anything to be done about it? Machiavelli does not provide a straightforward answer. In part, that is because he is unfamiliar with the terms of the problem. But it is also because, in his view, it is impossible to prescribe any remedy without knowing whether the society in question is corrupt.

For Machiavelli, corruption is destiny. As his analysis of the early history of Rome reveals, little harm can come to a republic unless it is corrupt, and little good if it is.[3] When the Roman kings, the Tarquins, were expelled, the republic was able to acquire and maintain its liberty; yet 465 years later when Caesar was killed, it could not. Such diverse outcomes can only be due to the fact that 'in the time of the Tarquins the Roman populace was not yet corrupt, but in the later period was extremely corrupt'.[4]

The obvious implication is that corruption must be avoided at all costs. But in the long run there is no escape, for corruption is the inevitable change wrought in states by time. All institutions, both religious and political, have something good in them at the start, but as the years go by they become increasingly corrupt unless something or someone intervenes to bring about renewal. A people that regains its freedom can keep it only if it is free from corruption, yet that freedom is often lost through the corruption of the very means by which it should be maintained, and, once established, corruption can never be reversed by normal methods.[5]

According to Machiavelli, corruption consists in esteeming the private more than the public good, and is caused by division into factions, which seek to benefit themselves, and so propose laws 'not for the sake of their common liberties, but to augment their own power'.[6] Factions are the result of idleness, and they feed off inequality, which is what created the divisions between patricians and plebs in republican Rome, and between the nobles and people (and later the rich and the poor) in medieval Florence.[7] Idleness therefore constitutes the turning point within the historical cycle in which the positive results of good government turn bad: 'Virtue is the mother of peace, peace produces idleness, idleness begets disorder, and disorder brings ruin.'[8]

In these circumstances, it is obviously vital to be able to tell whether a state is corrupt or not, and hence where it is in the cycle of corruption. And so in chapter 17 of the

Discourses Machiavelli offers what amounts to a diagnostic test:

> It is possible then to arrive at this conclusion: when the material is not corrupt, tumults and other troubles do no harm, but, when it is corrupt, good legislation is of no avail unless it be initiated by someone in so extremely strong a position that he can enforce obedience until such time as the material has become good.[9]

On this hypothesis, states that can withstand tumults without harm are not corrupt, whereas those that cannot reveal themselves to be riddled with corruption already. Proof is to be found in Livy's history, where absence of corruption is the reason that the numerous tumults that took place in Rome 'did no harm, but, on the contrary, were an advantage to that republic'.[10]

Rome: harmless tumults

As usual, Machiavelli relishes the counterintuitive conclusion and sets out to defend it. He imagines someone objecting that the tumults of ancient Rome were almost barbaric: 'Look how people used to assemble and clamour against the senate, and how the senate decried the people, how men ran helter-skelter about the streets. How the shops were closed, and how the plebs en masse would troop out of Rome.' Machiavelli's response is that it is a mistake to focus on the noise and commotion rather than what resulted from it. In every republic there is a division between 'the populace and that of the upper class and ... all legislation favourable to liberty is brought about by the clash between them'. Every city should therefore provide some outlet for the ambitions of the populace, especially if it hopes to involve them in military or other projects.[11]

Machiavelli here refers to the ongoing struggle between the patricians and the plebs in the Roman republic, and in particular to the first secession of the plebs in 494 BCE described by Livy. In the midst of a war against neighbouring tribes, mounting concern about crippling plebeian indebtedness resulted in the plebs refusing military service. Instead, they marched out of the city and they set up a fortified camp on the Mons Sacer, where they sat and waited to see what would happen. Alarmed by the situation, the senate agreed to negotiations which resulted in the creation of plebeian tribunes to represent the interests of the plebeians against the patrician consuls.[12]

Using this example, Machiavelli argues that the critics should judge by results: 'If tumults led to the creation of the tribunes, tumults deserve the highest praise.' A republic cannot be stigmatized as disordered if 'there occur such striking examples of virtue, since good examples proceed from good education, good education from good laws, and good laws in this case from those very tumults which many so inconsiderately condemn'. Indeed, Machiavelli goes further, arguing not only that the harmlessness of tumults shows the republic not to have been corrupt, but that without them Rome could not have achieved such greatness.[13]

Sparta and Venice: no tumults

In order to demonstrate the point, Machiavelli asks whether it would have been possible to set up a form of government that would have prevented these controversies. He therefore offers two examples of republics 'free from such animosities and tumults', one ancient and one modern: Sparta and Venice, both republics famous for their longevity and as such often held, by other political theorists of the Renaissance, to be enduring models of political virtue.[14]

Machiavelli's judgement is more nuanced. According to his (not wholly accurate) description, Sparta was governed by a king and a small senate, and scrupulously followed the laws of Lycurgus which prescribed equality of property (though not of rank). It had few inhabitants and immigration was forbidden. The plebs had no access to positions of authority but, having the support of the king (in whose interest it was to protect them from any injustice at the hands of the nobles) and enjoying equality of property, they had no incentive to seek it. According to Machiavelli, the exclusion of foreigners and the smallness of the population gave Sparta 'no chance either to become corrupt, or to become so unwieldy that it could no longer be managed by the few who governed it'.[15]

In Venice, too, there were no tumults because the original inhabitants retained power as a class, while making no distinctions among themselves. The city was governed by a mercantile elite who had successfully excluded the rest of the population from participation. Newcomers were without access to the complex machinery of politics, and in any case there were not enough of them to upset the balance of power. The predominance of the indigenous nobility was preserved not just by their relative numerical strength, but by their assiduous devotion to trade rather than gentlemanly idleness, and the fact that they did not use their own population in wars, but employed mercenaries instead.

Machiavelli therefore concludes that Rome's legislators would have had to do one of two things if Rome were to remain tranquil: 'either to emulate the Venetians and not employ its plebs in wars, or, like the Spartans, not to admit foreigners'. But by doing both, Rome allowed the plebs to increase in numbers and strength and so cause tumults. If it had done neither it would have been more tranquil, but also weaker, for 'in seeking to remove the causes of tumults, Rome would have removed also the causes of expansion'.[16] In Machiavelli's account, it is possible to arrange a state in such a way that tumults do not occur, but only by sacrificing the military manpower needed to expand, or to defend territory from hostile neighbours. For all their longevity, the power of the Venetian and Spartan republics proved in the end to be surprisingly brittle.

Florence: harmful tumults

Although he does not refer to it in the *Discourses*, Machiavelli has a third possibility in mind. There are not only states in which there are no tumults, or in which tumults do no harm, but also states in which tumults undermine the strength of the state from within. Here, the primary example is close to hand: Florence; and it is in the *Florentine Histories* that the potentially disastrous consequences of internal disorder are revealed.

The source of all this strife is faction.[17] And the underlying cause was, as it had been in Rome, the conflict between the nobles and the people that comes from 'the disposition of the one to command, and the indisposition of the other to obey'. The result was the same in both cases – one tumult after another. However, there were important differences between the two republics in this regard: tumults in Florence were more violent and undermined the republic's military potential; and whereas those in Rome led from an equality of citizens to inequality, those of Florence led from inequality to equality. According to Machiavelli, the crucial difference was that in Rome the plebeians sought to share control of the state with the patricians, whereas in Florence the people wanted it exclusively for themselves.[18]

Unlike other republics, which had only one social division, that between the nobles and the people, Florence had many. In Florence, inter-factional conflict never stopped because rather than tolerating opposition, the victors sought to destroy it. A faction remained united only for as long as was needed to defeat its opponents, and then divided against itself as soon as it had eliminated them.[19] The first division was among the nobles, afterwards between the nobles and the citizens, and finally between the citizens and the populace. Each successful group governed solely in its own interest and so inevitably spawned a new opposing faction.[20]

Tumult and corruption

Machiavelli maintains that the difference between corrupt and an uncorrupted states can be seen in the effect of tumults. In an uncorrupted state, tumults prevent corruption by creating new institutions; in a corrupt one, they accelerate it, by promoting violence between factions. But there is a potential contradiction here:

1) corruption is giving priority to factional interest
2) in an uncorrupted republic tumults do no harm
3) tumults give priority to factional interest
4) an uncorrupted republic is one where there is corruption

In order to run the tumult test at all, there must be enough corruption for tumults to arise. Where there are no tumults (as in Sparta and Venice) there is assumed to be no corruption either. Elsewhere, corruption and tumults increase together. According to Machiavelli, all institutions are prone to disintegration and in need of periodic renovation. If such upheavals do not happen regularly, there is more corruption, and with it more danger and more tumult.[21]

In the Roman republic, there was no discontinuity between tumults that led to renovation and tumults that were a symptom of corruption. On the contrary, the former led directly to the latter. Whenever the plebeians wanted something, they caused a tumult or refused to enlist in the army.[22] So the corruption of the Tarquins was corrected by their expulsion by the patricians; the corruption of the nobility by the tumults of the plebs, who then went on to create more tumults and make ever more demands.[23] Not satisfied with one consulship, the plebeians sought to have both, and after that 'the censorship, the praetorship and all the other great offices of the city'. Machiavelli attributes the final sequence of plebeian demands to the corruption with which populist leaders like the Gracchi brothers and Gaius Marius had impregnated the people.[24] But he misses the inference that earlier tumults must also have been due to partisanship (and hence corruption), and that between the Tarquins and the Gracchi republican Rome was not uncorrupted so much as a society with the right amount of corruption. (It is, however, implied in his statement in 1.6 that he plans to confine his discussion 'to peoples in whom corruption has not advanced too far, and in whom there is still more goodness than rottenness'.[25])

There is therefore an inherent ambiguity in Machiavelli's account in that corruption must be present in order to be shown to be absent. No republic can be free unless it is at least partly uncorrupted, but the tumult test cannot demonstrate that freedom unless the republic is also partly corrupt. The tumult test does not distinguish between the corrupt and the uncorrupt; it rather provides a measure of corruption. It is not an experiment but a sample. All of which suggests that corruption may be as responsible for the positive political transitions Machiavelli describes as for the negative ones. In which case perhaps corruption has a similar role to play in our own society and institutions.

Machiavelli in the postcolony

The problems of the early Roman republic may seem remote from those of modernity, and Machiavelli's interpretation of them (especially his emphasis on war and the need for territorial expansion) of little relevance to the contemporary nation-state. However, Machiavelli's account of corruption found new application in the first generation of scholarship in development studies, during a period in which the results of decolonization sometimes seemed to fulfil his expectation that a people liberated from foreign rule 'forthwith returns to the yoke'.[26] And this literature, read against the political grain of its sometimes conservative authors, provides an overlapping set of coordinates within which the contours of the present emerge more clearly.

In his essay 'Political Development and Political Decay' (1965), and in his later book *Political Order in Changing Societies* (1968), Samuel P. Huntington argued that politics is governed by 'the conflict between mobilization and institutionalization'. Political stability depends 'upon the ratio of institutionalization to participation', so when political participation increases as a result of social mobilization, a society's political institutions must adapt if stability is to be maintained. Without strong and adaptable institutions, increased mobilization will result in instability and violence.[27] This is a particular problem in the context of development when existing ethnic and religious groups are supplemented by professional and class alliances. It becomes more difficult to maintain order, because social mobilization easily outstrips the adaptation of political institutions, undermining traditional forms before new ones are established and functioning. Unless restrained, modernization and social mobilization therefore produce 'political decay'.[28]

Using mobilization and institutionalization as variables Huntington describes four ideal polities defined by whether institutionalization and mobilization are high or low: (1) those with high levels of both mobilization and institutionalization are 'modern, developed, civic polities'; (2) those with high mobilization and low institutionalization are corrupt polities; (3) those with high institutionalization and low mobilization are contained polities, while (4) those which have low levels of both are primitive polities.[29]

Social mobilization	Political institutionalization	
	High	*Low*
High	1. Civic	2. Corrupt
Low	3. Contained	4. Primitive

Huntington focuses particularly on polities with a low institutionalization to participation ratio where 'private ambitions are rarely restrained by public authority; [and] the role of power (ie wealth and force) is maximised'. He explicitly links this discussion of corrupt polities with Machiavelli's account of corruption, describing societies with weak political institutions as lacking both the ability 'to curb the excesses of personal and parochial desires' and the means to define and realize 'common interests'. The classic examples are provided by developing societies in which traditional institutions have withered or collapsed and the result is 'a corrupt polity with a high rate of participation but a low level of institutionalization'.[30]

This account as a whole maps easily onto Machiavelli's scheme, adding the perspectives of political sociology to an outline drawn from ancient politics. Not only is there a clear affinity between Huntington's corrupt polity and Machiavelli's account of the corruption of the Florentine Republic in which the mobilization of the various factions overwhelms the political institutions designed to represent them, but the analogy extends further. Republican Rome, where tumults do no harm, emerges as an example of what Huntington would have called a civic polity. With high levels of both institutionalization and mobilization, social mobilization results in institutional change, and new institutions are created (e.g., the plebeian tribunes) that productively channel future political participation. In contrast, Sparta and Venice would count as contained states (the former a monarchy, the latter an aristocracy) characterized by a near total absence of social mobilization, and the non-participation of the plebs in political life. Social control is exercised through the state and, in the case of Sparta, where men were obliged to eat together every day apart from their families, every other form of social tie that might compete with that of loyalty to the republic is rigorously excluded.

Taken together, the possible results of Machiavelli's Tumult Test would produce a matrix that looks like this:

	Political institutionalization	
Social mobilization	*High*	*Low*
High	Rome	Florence
Low	Sparta/Venice	

There are no tumults in contained polities where political institutions are strong and mobilization low; tumults do no harm in civic polities where there is a balance between the two, and tumults undermine the corrupt polities where the institutions are no match for the social forces that produce unrest. As a non-institutionalized form of political participation, tumult itself counts as a form of social mobilization, so one reason that tumults harm a corrupt state, in which, by definition, social mobilization already exceeds institutionalization, is that they threaten to tip the scales still further.

The index of corruption implied by this typology is the ratio of social mobilization to political institutionalization.

It is low in Sparta and Venice, productively balanced in republican Rome, excessively high in Florence. Machiavelli uses the concept of corruption to describe the transition from civic to corrupt polities, from ones where tumult is harmless or beneficial to ones where it is not. But the move from a republic without tumults (a contained state) to one where tumults are beneficial (a civic polity) must also involve social mobilization. In other words it is corruption, the growing ratio of private to public good, that propels the move from a state like Sparta or Venice to one like Rome, just as it propels the move from a republic like Rome to one like Florence.

How might this mobilization be described? In 'The "Soft State" in Underdeveloped Countries', Gunnar Myrdal identified developing nations in which this process had occurred as 'soft' rather than 'strong' states. Soft states were characterized by 'a general lack of social discipline … [and] a general inclination of people … to resist public controls and their implementation'.[31] In India, for example, Gandhi's technique of *satyagraha* had mobilized pre-existing communal loyalties against the colonial government, and left a legacy of 'anarchic attitudes which the new indigenous governments now [found] turned against themselves'.[32] Myrdal viewed the softening up of the Indian state as a danger to democracy, but as Amartya Sen later argued, it was this softening that prevented the repeated famines that occurred under the 'hard state' of colonial rule.[33]

In fact, a soft state may not necessarily mean a reduction in the overall level of social control. As Joel Migdal emphasized in *Strong Societies and Weak States* (1988) (written partly under Huntington's sponsorship, but substantially modifying his conclusions), endemic social indiscipline is not a function of personal deviance, but reflects an underlying conflict about whether it is the government or other organizations – families, ethnic groups, religions, business organizations, etc. – that set the norms. Social control may either be centralized by a strong state (in the narrow sense of the government and its institutions) that dominates a weak society, or fragmented among fairly autonomous social organizations that together create a strong society while leaving the coercive and administrative powers of the government relatively weak.[34] Softening up the state as a whole involves a transfer from one normative framework to another. But it does not always bring ruin. Corruption can bring transformation as well as disaster.

Between Venice and Rome

What might Machiavelli's tumult test reveal today? The 1990s saw considerable social unrest in China, Mexico, Indonesia and Thailand, and the past two decades have been a period of increasing tumults worldwide. Global studies conducted in 2013 and 2020 found a broadly similar pattern: although subject to considerable local variation, political protests were both increasing in number from year to year, and growing larger in size. Between 2009 and 2019, the number of anti-government protests globally increased at an annual rate of 11.5 percent, and in the final years of that decade the rate of increase was particularly marked in the advanced economies of the capitalist core (which had seemed relatively immune during the earlier period), with the five largest demonstrations in US history all taking place during the Trump presidency.[35]

These developments are not the result of chance. As Wolfgang Streeck has argued, they reflected the inherent contradiction of 'democratic capitalism', which is 'a political economy ruled by two conflicting principles, or regimes, of resource allocation: one operating according to marginal productivity, or what is revealed as merit by a "free play of market forces", and the other based on social need or entitlement, as certified by the collective choices of democratic politics'. Governments have tried various expedients (toleration of inflation, acceptance of public debt and deregulation of private credit) to reconcile the two principles, but the normal condition of democratic capitalism is conflict between the markets and democratic politics.

The inevitable consequence is that insofar as governments align themselves with the market, they will be forced to curtail forms of democratic expression liable to disrupt the smooth operation of market forces. The result is that citizens are 'stripped of their democratic defences and their capacity to impress upon the political economy interests and demands that are incommensurable with those of capital owners'. According to Streeck, this means that the only way to keep the market in check is through 'street riots and popular insurrection ... the last remaining mode of political expression for those devoid of market power'.[36]

However, as Karl Polanyi pointed out many years ago, the market economy is 'more allergic to rioting than any other economic system we know'. In the early modern period, governments tolerated riots as a means of making grievances public, but with the rise of the market attitudes hardened. Every hint of public disorder was a potential threat to stock prices, and an 'affray in the streets of the metropolis might destroy a substantial part of the nominal national capital'. Capital could never be secure unless all forces that might set aside the rules of the market 'were eliminated from the political scene'.[37] A 'market state' (i.e., one that makes market efficiency the sole normative criterion) always aspires to be a contained state, where the government is strong and society weak. However, rather than trying to uphold and enforce traditional social and legal norms, it has a system of incentives and penalties designed 'to prevent the social instability that threatens material well-being'.[38]

As the theorists of neo-liberalism recognized from the start, politics itself is liable to distort the market. According to Milton Friedman, 'the fundamental defect of the political mechanism [i.e., democracy] is that it is a system of highly weighted voting under which the special interests have great incentive to promote their own interests at the expense of the general public.'[39] Simply by putting together a coalition to form a majority, factions can take control of governments for their own benefit while making everyone pay the costs. It is the market, where everyone pays their own way and has an interest in receiving value for money, that more effectively represents the general interest.

It is easy to see how Friedman's equation of spending money with voting translates into what Streeck calls 'the economic democracy of capitalism – one dollar, one vote' in which the economic interests of those with market power is equated with the general interest.[40] The market state

(Streeck's 'consolidation state') is a contained state, but one of a peculiar kind, a plutocracy in which the public interest is the aggregated outcome of private exchange, and political participation has become, almost by definition, a form of corruption, for it must represent some private or factional interest rather than the public good of the market. The ideal market state is, like Venice, a plutocracy untroubled by politics; but in recent years, the market state has become more like Rome, a plutocracy tempered by riots.

Corruption from below

Are market states corrupt enough to sustain this level of tumult in the long term? Machiavelli was preoccupied with making Florence more like Rome, and does not consider how the Venetian republic might have become more like the Roman one. But he does identify the conditions under which a state is left uncorrupted and undisturbed, and it is possible to see how these conditions might be reversed to achieve the opposite result.

The key to the unruffled stability of Sparta and Venice was the exclusion of outsiders. Sparta did everything it could to prevent foreigners from settling and intermarrying, while Venice excluded newcomers from all political rights. The first condition of increased social mobilization is therefore openness to inward migration. According to Machiavelli, 'there are two ways of acquiring this large population, by friendliness and by force. It is done by friendliness when the road is kept open and safe for foreigners who propose to come and dwell there so that everyone is glad to do so.' Rome used both methods and grew accordingly; it therefore 'appears to have been more tumultuous and not so well governed as they [Athens and Sparta] were'.[41] However, immigration may not be enough. According to Machiavelli, the usual cause of disunity in a republic is 'idleness and peace'.[42] If a nation 'has no need to go to war, it will then come about that idleness will either render it effeminate or give rise to factions; and these two things, either in conjunction or separately, will bring about its downfall'.[43] The process is facilitated by Christianity, a 'religion of idleness' which promotes contemplative indolence and has failed to instil martial virtues.[44]

Friendliness to foreigners and increased idleness: these two seemingly undemanding requirements should, according to Machiavelli, be enough to ensure factions and tumults, for immigrants usually find themselves in a disadvantageous position relative to the original inhabitants, and this forms the basis of social division. Idleness furnishes the time and opportunity needed to form factions and create tumults – not just the tumults that bring harm but (though Machiavelli misses this point) those needed to achieve renewal or change as well. Might Machiavelli's formula for corruption be applicable to contemporary Western democracies, and if so, what would be the case for adopting it?

Keeping the road open and safe for potential migrants is not currently a priority in Europe or the Anglosphere, but the argument for doing so can be made quite independently of Machiavelli. Not only are current border controls ineffective, but there is a strong case for open borders on both egalitarian and libertarian grounds. Given that the most dramatic economic inequalities are between rather than within nations, and that migration and the resulting remittances are one of the most effective ways to address inequality, it is hard to see how any egalitarian can ignore the need for more immigration to the wealthy countries of the global North.[45] More fundamentally, there seems no logical reason why people should be denied freedom of movement not just within but between nations, rather than being constrained by arbitrary physical and political boundaries that significantly impact their life-chances and capacity for self-determination.[46]

With the decline of monasticism, the religious case for idleness has less currency than it once did. But in the market state where every minute of the day has been colonized by capitalism, the right to do nothing, to be inattentive, or even just sleep, has taken on an enhanced significance.[47] The idea of a universal basic income has been proposed as a simple, efficient and egalitarian alternative to existing forms of welfare provision. It also has the effect of rebalancing attitudes towards employment in favour of affective labour and self-development. And while it is unlikely to persuade most people to give up their jobs, it removes the stigma of idleness with a government subsidy and provides a new basis for the freedom from work which strands of both libertarian and Marxist thought have long seen as desirable.[48]

Immigration and the future of the welfare state are two key areas of long-term policy debate in Western democracies. Within these debates open borders and basic income are live options that are gaining traction across traditional political divides. However, the two policies are usually discussed separately because of uncertainty about their potential combined effect. Machiavelli encourages us to put them together and see what is at stake. It is often assumed than combining open borders with basic income would be impractical because of the welfare-magnet effect. The available evidence suggests any such effect might be more limited than anticipated, but there is no doubt that there would be additional opportunities for free-riding.[49] Open borders and basic income would mean more immigration and more idleness, and, very probably, more idle immigrants.

From one point of view therefore, Machiavelli's formula for corruption looks like a strategy for filling a country with unemployed immigrants so that they can riot in the streets. The most articulate advocates of this perspective, Samuel Huntington himself and the conservative journalist Christopher Caldwell, believe that even existing immigration and welfare policies produce a factious alien population lacking a work ethic.[50] Machiavelli would not entirely dismiss their arguments. But rather than asking, as Caldwell's subtitle does, 'Can Europe Be the Same with Different People in It?', Machiavelli might ask 'Can Europe Be Different with the Same People in It?'

In order for a contained state to be transformed into a civic polity, it needs softening up. Whereas Huntington's model envisages social mobilization in developing countries as coming about through the growth of new professional and economic groups to supplement traditional social divisions, social mobilization in the market state is more likely to occur through the emergence of new ethnic and religious groupings that supplement existing economic divisions demobilized and resubordinated by neo-liberalism. In contemporary Europe, what Machiavelli would have called tumults already rely heavily on the participation of second-generation immigrants and the economically inactive (i.e., students and the unemployed).[51] The strong correlation between unemployment and ethnicity itself provides a reason for protest, but both factors taken independently may also be said to enable it, confirming Machiavelli's supposition that faction is a prerequisite for tumult, not just in providing shared motivation, but also in furnishing individuals with community support.[52]

Recent research by Carew Boulding, revisiting Huntington's hypothesis on the relationship between political institutions and social mobilization in a South American context, confirms that rather than always fostering moderate collaboration with the institutions of the state or, conversely, being inherently destabilizing and liable to lead to mob rule or civil war, social mobilization has different impacts depending on the political context. It may, rather as Machiavelli argued, both harm or support the state depending on the quality of its political institutions. Indeed, Boulding points out that 'as long as the government remains above a threshold for democracy', 'even very contentious political action … often builds support for democratic systems'.[53] This suggests that in a contained state that is at least residually democratic, tumult is always beneficial rather than harmful for it will either promote popular legislative change, or – even when it fails in that ambition, or indeed lacks it altogether – further the social mobilization that is the precondition of achieving it in the future. Rather than pointing to the conclusion that tumult is pointless, a reading of Machiavelli suggests that it is in a contained state that tumult is liable to have the most beneficial effect.

Machiavelli is distinguished not by seeing antagonism as inescapable, but by regarding it as to some degree desirable. Far from demonstrating that conflict is a permanent feature of every state, he emphasizes that there have been republics free of 'animosities and tumults' like Sparta and Venice, and describes the mechanisms through which tumults were avoided. His contemporary relevance therefore lies in showing how it might be possible to escape containment and make a transition away from the market state. But as usual, taking on board Machiavelli's advice requires a degree of reorientation. For critics of capitalism, it is axiomatic that the market state is corrupt and in need of reform. Machiavelli suggests a different response – that it is not corrupt enough, and in need of softening up.

6
Slack

Environmentalists are always saying that human beings should consume less of the planet's natural resources. In some cases this involves the temporary or permanent non-use of a specific resource; in others, a reduction in the level of its consumption. The latter may involve resource substitution, the absolute or relative decoupling of economic growth from resource use, or else the adoption of policies designed to limit or reduce growth itself. In all cases, however, the result is the same. Irrespective of whether the goal is an overall reduction in the human consumption of natural resources or merely their more intelligent allocation, the effect of environmentalist policies is to ensure that some resources that could be used are left unexploited, and that a gap opens up between potential and actual levels of resource use.

What sort of political ideal does this represent? Save in those instances where capping use at any one time is necessary to maximize use across time, the non-use of usable resources is, by most standards, sub-optimal if not down-right irrational. Those environmentalists who consciously advocate global strategies of this kind (as opposed to the short-term, targeted conservation of specific resources) often do so on the basis of a non-anthropocentric ethics where what is best for the planet takes precedence over what is best for human beings. In consequence, there has been little focus on the idea of suboptimality itself, or on its historical parallels and antecedents.

By looking at the arguments that led to the acceptance of non-use value within environmental economics in the United States in the mid-twentieth century, and at the contemporaneous development of the concept of 'organizational slack', it is possible to get a clearer sense of the intellectual traditions to which these arguments relate. Slack was defined by Albert O. Hirschman as a gap between actual and potential performance, and in his account becomes closely aligned with the chronic under-use of political resources that Machiavelli termed corruption. Could the non-use of natural resources then be seen as a form of idleness akin to Machiavelli's corruption, and if so, from what perspective might such idleness appear a constructive political strategy?

Idle resources

Within the field of environmental economics, the first person to advocate the non-use of natural resources appears to have been the Dartmouth College economist L. Gregory Hines. At the Eighteenth North American Wildlife Conference in 1953, he presented a paper entitled 'The Myth of Idle Resources: A Reconsideration of the Concept of

Nonuse in Conservation'. It had, he complained, 'become commonplace … to point out that conservation does not imply the nonuse or idleness of resources'. To an alarming degree, 'emphasis upon full use or "full employment" of all resources' had diverted attention from the appropriate use for given resources, and afforded 'a basis for attack upon conservation programs by those who wish to bring all resources under commercial exploitation'.[1] It was, instead, Hines's contention that

> the needs of mankind cannot be revealed and met within the perimeters of the market economy alone, but require conscious appraisal of social goals and the means of obtaining them. High in the scheme of social goals to fulfil basic human needs must be a definite provision for idle resources – idle to permit replenishment of productivity and to provide an emergency buffer for a future that seems more uncertain than ever before.[2]

As Hines explained, the problem with the market is that the pricing system simultaneously 'fails to restrict commercial utilization of some resources that should remain idle, [and] provides no effective means by which an individual can express his desire for commercial nonuse'. The lack of 'a socially adequate criterion for resource allocation' applies both to wilderness as 'a unique antidote to the pace of a highly industrialized civilization' and to 'renewable resources … [which] may require periodic disuse or idleness to preserve a given level of productivity through time'.[3]

The myth to which Hines refers had several strands. One was embodied in government thinking about conservation after the First World War. In the late nineteenth century, John Muir, the pioneer of American environmentalism, had argued for the preservation of natural environments in absolute terms. Believing that 'every natural artefact is a reflection of the beauty, magnificence and abundance of the Creator', Muir thought of nature as 'God's first temple'. It was therefore axiomatic that it should receive similar respect. Muir likened the sheep grazing around Shadow Lake to the money-changers in the temple, and when, in 1908, it was proposed that Hetch Hetchy Valley in California should be flooded to create a reservoir for San Francisco, he responded: 'As well dam for water-tanks the people's cathedrals and churches, for no holier temple has ever been consecrated by the heart of man.'[4]

But Muir lost the battle over Hetch Hetchy to his fellow environmentalist and former friend, Gifford Pinchot, the chief of the United States Forest Service.[5] To Muir's ideal of 'preservation' Pinchot had counterposed the idea of 'conservation', by which he understood 'the greatest good of the greatest number for the longest time'. On this view, 'the first principle of conservation is development, the use of natural resources on this continent for the benefit of the people who live here now' and the second is the 'prevention of waste'. However, the two were not entirely distinct, for Pinchot considered that 'there may be just as much waste in neglecting the development and use of certain natural resources as there is in their destruction'.[6]

It was on the basis of this philosophy that the 'myth of idle resources' developed. Speaking in his later role as governor of Pennsylvania on Conservation Day in 1926, Pinchot said:

We have vast stretches of idle forest land. It brings no good to anyone. It pays little or no taxes, keeps willing hands out of work, builds no roads, supports no industries, kills railroads, depopulates towns, creates a migratory population, all of which work against a good and stable citizenship. Idle forest serves no one well. It is a menace to our normal national life.[7]

The address was frequently reprinted and quoted in the following decades in order to sustain the argument that 'We need to ... put idle forest land to work.'[8] But during the Depression, the concern with idle forests came to intersect with wider anxiety about the idleness of resources. Now idle land was just one element in the litany of idleness: 'a composite of idle men, idle land, idle machines and idle money'.[9] In line with Keynes's view that the remedy for the trade cycle was to be found not in abolishing booms but in abolishing slumps, popular writers such as Stuart Chase imagined how all of America's idle resources might be employed in future public works:

We have idle money and we have idle men. This world we have sketched can use them to the last dollar and the last man. Great sections of the American landscape must be torn down, redesigned, rebuilt; and this will demand intensive investment on a colossal scale.[10]

The US government largely agreed. There was, as the US Department of Agriculture Forest Service stated in 1941, 'a great need and opportunity to put idle men and idle land to work again'.[11]

By mid-century, therefore, it appeared that the Muir-Pinchot debate had been settled decisively in Pinchot's favour. Even before the Depression, his policy of achieving a sustainable yield from the national forests had taken priority over the ideal of preserving the American wilderness. But with the spread of Keynesian ideas in response to the economic crisis, this approach gained a wider economic rationale. The idleness of land was taken to be another example of what Keynes considered capitalism's 'chronic tendency to the under-employment of resources'.[12] It was therefore the government's duty to ensure the full employment of a nation's natural resources just as much as its human ones. As Ezra Taft Benson, Eisenhower's secretary of agriculture, said to the AFA Fourth American Forest Congress in October 1953, 'I hope we no longer have any citizens who look upon conservation and preservation as synonymous terms ... [We must not] fail to make the land yield up to its full potential of the resource for which it is best fitted.'[13]

The defence of idleness

Hines's defence of idleness may not be couched in religious terms like that of Muir, but it derives in part from Muir's follower Aldo Leopold, who had developed a less mystical version of the argument for the non-exploitation of natural resources in his 1949 essay 'The Land Ethic'. Although referring to 'conservation' rather than 'preservation', Leopold distinguished between the different attitudes to conservation represented by group (A), which regards 'the land as soil, and its function as commodity-production'

and 'is quite content to grow trees like cabbages', and group
(B), which 'regards the land as a biota, and its function as
something broader', and so 'worries about whole series
of secondary forest functions: wildlife, recreation, water-
sheds, wilderness areas'. In Leopold's opinion, any system
of conservation which assumed that the 'economic parts of
the biotic clock will function without the uneconomic parts'
was mistaken.[14]

Hines echoes Leopold's view, but he writes as an economist, and seeks to develop an account of how those
'uneconomic parts' function within the economy of the
whole. In this respect, his critique of full employment resonates with the arguments not just of ecologists, but of
anti-Keynesian economists. Even in the Depression there
were some who argued against the Keynesian view that full
employment should be maintained and that idle resources
were necessarily undesirable. In *The Theory of Idle Resources*
(1939) William Hutt argued that 'full employment', in the
sense of a 'wasteless economy', was neither a definable nor
a desirable goal.[15] According to Hutt, value and use must be
distinguished because there are many ways in which what
looks like non-productive idleness may actually be very
productive, indeed essential to the smooth working of the
system.

Primarily concerned with employment, Hutt argued that
in this regard there was no distinction between the idleness
of labour and the idleness of other resources. In his opinion, it was obvious that 'in any given state of knowledge
and institutions, there are resources which perform their
most wanted services through their mere passive existence,

the service of availability'. Such 'pseudo-idleness ... exists when resources are being retained in their specialized form ... because the productive service of carrying them through time is being performed', because no other value (e.g., their scrap or hire value) will exceed their capital value at some future time.[16]

Although Hines makes no direct reference to Hutt's work in 'The Myth of Idle Resources', he offers a similar argument against the 'full employment' of natural resources on the basis that 'wilderness ... yields social returns that become greater with each increase in population, extension of cultivation, and mechanization of production ... [and] will increase in social value, undoubtedly at a progressive rate, as our economy continues to expand'.[17] As he explained in an earlier article, 'Wilderness Areas: An Extra Market Problem in Resource Allocation', 'for wilderness to be most useful to society, it must remain unused in the traditional commercial sense because such an area has greater economic value in its primitive state' not least because the gain from grazing rights (Hutt's 'hire value') will never be greater than the loss from destruction of top soil and the elimination of plants and animals.[18] Though less sonorous than Muir's denunciation of sheep as the money-changers to be driven from the temple, Hines's argument that hire value will never exceed future capital value in wilderness areas has the same effect.

In Hines's account, the economic value of 'non-use' is affirmed without any explicit argument as to why it will increase at a progressive rate, or how that value should be quantified. But in 'Conservation Reconsidered' (1967), another environmental economist, John Krutilla, specifies both. The value of an unused natural resource may be calculated in terms of the minimum that would be required to compensate those who enjoy or appreciate its existence in an unspoiled natural state ('the spiritual descendants of John Muir') for its loss in perpetuity. Over time, this value is likely to exceed the value to be derived from commercial exploitation because the inelasticity of natural resources means that 'the marginal trade-off between manufactured and natural amenities will progressively favor the latter', while 'the learn-by-doing phenomenon' will simultaneously allow more people to acquire the knowledge and skills needed to access and appreciate natural amenities and so change tastes in their favour. The conjunction of the two means that 'natural environments will represent irreplaceable assets of appreciating value with the passage of time'.[19]

Krutilla's claim that conservation 'requires a present action (which may violate conventional benefit-cost criteria) to be compatible with the attainment of future states of affairs', aligns it with Hutt's definition of 'pseudo-idleness' which exists 'whenever resources are withheld from immediately more profitable specialization or despecialization because of expectations of a different situation in the future'.[20] And Krutilla maintains that such option value may exist 'even though there is no current intention to use the area or facility in question and the option may never be exercised', rather in the way that Hutt says unutilized domestic goods such as a fire extinguisher may bring '*continuous* satisfactions simply through my knowledge that they are there'.[21]

For Muir, non-use had been a spiritual imperative, and for Leopold it had been an ecological one; but for Krutilla and subsequent environmental economists, non-use has a value that can be specified in economic terms. It is clear that in the transition from the transcendental value Muir ascribed to nature to the development of economists' accounts of non-use value, Hines and other defenders of idleness played a pivotal role. But in order to appreciate the wider intellectual context in which this transition took place, it is helpful to track contemporary developments in both macro- and microeconomics.

Slack

Whether articulated in terms of idle resources or non-use values, the policies of non-exploitation advocated by environmentalists have an obvious, though unremarked, affinity with another concept that emerges over the same time period – first in macroeconomics, and then in organization theory. During the 1940s (and perhaps before) one word that was frequently used to sum up the litany of 'idle men, idle machines, idle money' was 'slack'.[22] With the onset of war, the value of this unused capacity became more apparent. As the economist T. W. Schultz testified to the Select Committee Investigating National Defense Migration in 1941:

> Our defense program has had at least one happy result. It has taught us how exceedingly large our unused capacity was. We had not only idle acres but idle resources of almost every kind – labor, plants, finance, technical knowledge, organization and management

capacity – a large supply of each waiting to be put to use. Because
of this slack, it has been possible thus far to actually produce both
more butter and guns.[23]

However, it was not until the first two Economic Reports of
the President in the Kennedy administration that the question
of slack received more focused attention. In the 1961 report,
there was an entire subsection on 'The Problem of Chronic
Slack and Full Recovery' in which it was stated that 'economic recovery ... is far more than a cyclical problem. It is
also a problem of chronic slack in the economy – the growing
gap between what we can and what we do produce.'[24] And in
1962, the received wisdom that 'periods of slack and reces-
sion in economic activity lead to idle machines as well as idle
men' was once again repeated.[25]

The appearance of the phrase 'chronic slack' in the *Economic Reports* ensured that the term had wide currency
during the Kennedy presidency. But although the second
report acknowledged that the slack economy of the previous year meant that 'additional demand from both private
and public sources was readily converted into increased production',[26] this was not translated into an appreciation of
the benefits of slack itself. Most commentators echoed the
1961 report in supposing that all will 'look ahead to the day
when the slack will be taken up and high levels of output and
employment will again be the norm'.[27]

At a microeconomic level, however, 'idle capacity' was
already being reinterpreted as 'organizational slack', and
interpreted more positively. The concept of 'organizational
slack' was first developed in a journal article by Richard M.

Cyert and James G. March in 1956, but it was only when represented in their book *A Behavioral Theory of the Firm* (1963) that it gained wider attention. Cyert and March defined slack as 'the allocation of organizational resources to the satisfaction of subunits in excess of the minimum required for maintenance of the system'. In practice this meant that 'significant amounts of individual energies potentially utilizable by the organization are, in fact, being directed to the satisfaction of other roles'.[28]

Cyert and March enumerated some of the forms that slack might take within the firm: the payment of excessive dividends to stockholders; prices set too low or wages too high; subunits allowed to expand without generating additional revenue; excessive executive compensation, and the provision of unnecessary public services.[29] None of these things might in themselves be aligned with organizational goals, but as Cyert and March point out, the slack so-created nevertheless represented 'a cushion ... [which] absorbs a substantial share of the potential variability in the firm's environment'. Slack therefore operates 'to stabilize the system in two ways: (1) by absorbing excess resources, it retains upward adjustment of aspirations in good times; (2) by providing a pool of emergency resources, it permits aspirations to be maintained (and achieved) during relatively bad times'.[30]

The essential ambivalence of slack has remained one of its defining characteristics in the specialist literature.[31] Given that slack means that organizations and individuals are refraining 'from using all the resources available to them', it necessarily 'describes a tendency not to operate at peak efficiency'.[32] It can therefore be viewed as 'synonymous with waste and as a reflection of managerial self-interest, incompetence and sloth'.[33] On the other hand, without slack 'a company cannot survive in an unstable environment, because the slack acts as a buffer against shock ... [and] enables a company to take risks and promote innovative behaviour'.[34]

Although now very extensive, the literature on slack produced within the context of organizational theory and management studies has had limited impact beyond those fields, and none at all within environmental thought. Nevertheless the analogies are clear enough. Not only did the concept of slack originally include 'idle land' along with 'idle men and idle machines', but the defining characteristic of slack – the non-use of usable resources – is precisely that enjoined by environmental economists from Hines onwards. For Hines too, idle resources were required 'to permit replenishment of productivity and to provide an emergency buffer for a future that seems more uncertain than ever before'.[35]

Slack, corruption and idleness

In *Exit, Voice and Loyalty* (1970), Albert O. Hirschman picks up the concept of slack from Cyert and March, links it to Herbert Simon's idea of 'satisficing' (not seeking the best possible outcome, but one that meets some acceptable threshold), and then applies it more widely. Describing slack as 'a gap of a given magnitude between actual and potential performance of individuals, firms, and organisations', Hirschman contrasts it with the 'image of a

relentlessly *taut economy* [which] has held a privileged place
in economic analysis'. He argues 'not only that slack has
somehow come into the world and exists in given amounts,
but that it is *continuously being generated* as a result of some
sort of entropy characteristic of human, surplus-producing
societies'. On this view, 'firms and other organizations
are conceived to be permanently and randomly subject to
decline and decay, that is, to a gradual loss of rationality,
efficiency, and surplus-producing energy'.[36]

Hirschman acknowledged that there was an affinity between his understanding of slack and Machiavelli's
account of corruption (*corruzione*). Asked 'How much community spirit does liberal society require?', he rephrased the
question as 'How can society avoid the ever present dangers
coming from what Machiavelli called *corruzione*?' and noted
that 'contemporary analysts have rediscovered these dangers and attempted to discuss them under more neutral or
technical labels such as "slack"'.[37] He does not elaborate on
this, though he later characterizes Machiavelli's *corruzione*
as 'the loss of public spirit, the exclusive concentration of
individual effort on personal or sectional interests'.[38] This
not only echoes Machiavelli's emphasis on the need 'to live
without factions, [and] to esteem the private less than the
public good', but aligns it with Cyert and March's account
of slack being produced when energies are 'directed to the
satisfaction of other roles (e.g., clique member, husband)
within which individual members of the business organization operate'.[39]

Hirschman read Machiavelli throughout his life, and
would therefore have been aware of Machiavelli's emphasis

on the role of idleness in the corruption of the state.[40] According to Machiavelli, the usual cause of disunity in a republic is 'idleness (*ozio*) and peace', for if a nation 'has no need to go to war, it will then come about that idleness will either render it effeminate or give rise to factions; and these two things, either in conjunction or separately, will bring about its downfall'.[41] Machiavelli's most sustained exposition of this theme appears in the first book of the *Discourses on Livy*:

> Since men work either of necessity or by choice, and since there is to be found to be greater virtue where choice has less to say to it, the question arises whether it would be better to choose a barren place in which to build cities so that men would have to be industrious and less given to idleness, and so would be more united because, owing to the poor situation, there would be less occasion for discord.

Machiavelli's answer to the question is that, if men did not try to gain dominion over each other, the former would be more advisable. However, since no community is able to develop independently without also having to defend itself against its neighbours, the latter is preferable. There can be no security without power, and power comes from establishing a city in a fertile place where it has scope to grow. The city then has the resources both to defend itself from enemy attack, and to conquer those who stand in the way of its expansion:

> As to the idleness which such a situation may encourage, it must be provided for by laws imposing that need to work which the situation does not impose. It is advisable here to follow the example

of those wise folk who have dwelt in most beautiful and fertile lands, ie in such lands as tend to produce idleness and ineptitude for training in virtue of any kind, and who, in order to obviate the disasters which the idleness induced by the amenities of the land might cause, have imposed the need for training on those who were to become soldiers, and have made this training such that men there have become better soldiers than those in countries which were rough and sterile by nature.

Machiavelli therefore concludes that 'it is more prudent to place a city in a fertile situation, provided its fertility is kept in due bounds by laws'.[42]

Hirschman's account of slack is developed in the same terms. Most human societies (unlike primate societies) are characterized by 'the existence of surplus over subsistence', and

the wide latitude [they] have for deterioration is the inevitable counterpart of man's increasing productivity and control over his environment. Occasional decline as well as prolonged mediocrity – in relation to achievable performance levels – must be accounted among the many penalties of progress.[43]

On this view, economic progress and latitude for deterioration are positively rather than negatively correlated. According to Hirschman, this accounts for

man's fundamentally ambivalent attitude toward his ability to produce a surplus ... while unwilling to give up progress he hankers after the simple rigid constraints on behaviour that governed him when he ... was totally absorbed by the need to satisfy his most basic drives.[44]

Machiavelli's suggestion that those who live in fertile lands must have 'laws imposing that need to work which the situation does not impose' would count as an example of this pattern. But so too would the reaction of those who in the modern economy 'search for ways and means to take up the slack, to retrieve the ideal of the taut economy'. Hirschman describes various 'pressure mechanisms' through which 'additional investment, hours of work, productivity, and decision making can be squeezed out'. If the pressures of competition prove insufficient, then the 'pressures of adversity will be invoked', exogenous forces such as strikes, war and revolution. For advocates of social revolution, for example, 'only revolutionary changes can tap and liberate the abundant but dormant, repressed or alienated energies of the people'.[45]

However, Hirschman argues, the search for pressure mechanisms can be mistaken, for slack may be a blessing in disguise. Slack permits firms to ride out adverse market conditions, and contributes to the stability and flexibility of political systems. As he indicates later in the book, 'for voice to function properly it is necessary that individuals possess reserves of political influence which they can bring into play', which requires that there be 'considerable slack in political systems'.[46] The artificial attempt to reproduce the conditions of necessity through pressure mechanisms may succeed only in squeezing out the slack that is necessary for reform and the long-term health of the state.

To this, Machiavelli's retort would probably be the same as the one he offers to Christian reformers, namely that by allowing slack, reform becomes increasingly difficult. This, he suggests, is what had happened in the Italy of his own time where the failure to instil martial virtues had inhibited active citizenship. This was the fault of 'those who have interpreted our religion in terms of idleness not in terms of virtue'. Whereas pagan religion had glorified army commanders and princes, 'our religion has glorified humble and contemplative men, rather than men of action. It has assigned as man's highest good humility, abnegation, and contempt for mundane things.'[47] In consequence, its prophets come unarmed.[48] Not just Savonarola, but also the original Dominicans and Franciscans who, Machiavelli complains, 'prevented the depravity of prelates and of religious heads from bringing ruin on religion' yet also taught that it was 'a good thing to live under obedience to such prelates' and so permitted the perpetuation of the very abuses they sought to reform.[49]

Machiavelli does not see idleness as ambivalent, only as a creator of discord, and as part of the cycle of corruption he describes in the *Florentine Histories*:

> Change is the lot of all things human and when they reach their utmost perfection and can ascend no higher they must of necessity decline. So, too, when they have sunk to the lowest point, and can sink no lower they begin to rise … Virtue is the mother of peace, peace produces idleness, idleness begets disorder, and disorder brings ruin. So order springs out of ruin, virtue out of order, and then follows a glorious fortune.[50]

Hirschman would not necessarily have disagreed with this sequence, for in *Shifting Involvements* (1982) he developed his own cyclical account of the oscillation of private interest and public action in modern societies, within which disappointment with and disengagement from the public sphere allows attention to be diverted to the pursuit of private interest and vice versa.[51] Unlike Machiavelli, who valued only public life, Hirschman presents private interest as the foundation of commercial society and gives equal weight to both spheres of action. Disengagement from one sphere permits the re-investment of resources in the other, so that, for example, exit from the private sphere may facilitate voice in the public one.

Although Hirschman does not use the world 'slack' in *Shifting Involvements* or refer back to Machiavelli's cycle of corruption and renovation, it is clear that the transfer from public to the private corresponds both to Hirschman's definition of Machiavelli's *corruzione* as 'loss of public spirit, [and] the exclusive concentration of individual effort on personal or sectional interests', and to Cyert and March's account of slack being produced when energies are 'directed to the satisfaction of other roles'. What the 'Hirschman cycle' demonstrates is that slack provides the latitude needed not only to meet unexpected problems, but to redirect resources to other objectives altogether.

By expanding the concept of slack to encompass the various ways in which social bodies may be 'permanently and randomly subject to decline and decay', Hirschman enables it to fulfil both the specific role of idleness in Machiavelli's account, and the larger one Machiavelli assigns to corruption in a world where 'human affairs are ever in a state of flux and cannot stand still'. But Hirschman always retains Cyert and March's insistence that the effects of slack are not exclusively deleterious. Whereas Machiavelli sees idleness as both a form and a source of corruption, slack is a form of corruption that permits renovation because it can furnish the idle resources needed to achieve renewal or change. Machiavelli seems to miss this possibility. In his account, order arises from ruin only because when things cannot get any worse they must get better; idleness is a step on the road to ruin, but has no equivalent role in the ascending part of the cycle. Although seemingly a welcome benefit of peace and surplus production, idleness leads only to disorder. Machiavelli has no sense that it might also be the means through which the cycle of corruption is arrested and renovation begun. But what sort of idea is that? And where does it come from?

Decadence and renewal

It is easy to find such thinking around the *fin de siècle* when, according to Frank Kermode, 'decadence and renewal [were] indistinguishable, or rather contemporaneous'.[52] For W. B. Yeats, 'the end of an age, which always receives the revelation of the character of the next age, is represented by the coming of one gyre to its place of greatest expansion and of the other to its place of greatest contraction'.[53] The spatial configuration Yeats envisages is formed by double vortices with the apex of one at the base of the other, so that the forms assumed by the 'inrushing gyre' take their shape from the contrary movement of the other.

As Yeats acknowledges, the idea that 'our civilisation was about to reverse itself or some new civilization was about to be born from all that our age had rejected' could be traced back to the work of the twelfth-century interpreter of the apocalypse, Joachim of Fiore.[54] Joachim conceived of history in terms of the Christian doctrine of the Trinity (the three *status* of the Father, Son and Holy Spirit) and argued that the interpenetration of the members of the Godhead indicated periods of overlap between one *status* and the next. Each *status* itself contains a sequence of germination, fructification and consummation, and so the consummation or decay of the first *status* is simultaneously the fructification of the second, and so on. One consequence of this is that the tribulation that marks the end of every age coincides with the coming of a new age, so that the transition between the two has a double aspect.[55]

Machiavelli's cyclical account of corruption and renovation, derived from the Roman historian Polybius, is a rejection of the apocalyptic mode of thought that had nearly triumphed in Savonarola's Florence. As J. G. A. Pocock observes,

> the air of Florence was heavy with apocalyptic, and Machiavelli could not have been as impervious to it as he may have liked to pretend. Innovation at the highest level, the creation of a just and stable society, had been attempted under the protection of the greatest concepts of Christian thought – nature, grace, prophecy and renovation; and the attempt had failed, so that it must have been falsely conceived.[56]

Not all of this apocalyptic speculation was directly inspired by Joachim, but 'the Joachimist marriage of woe and exaltation exactly fitted the mood', and Savonarola's expectation that God would renew his church with the sword of tribulation was characteristic of it.[57] Rather than missing the possibility that decline and renewal might happen together, Machiavelli rejected it by emphasizing that unarmed prophets do not succeed and that renovation requires political action rather than divine grace. He merely mocked the idea that 'Without you for you God fights / While you are on your knees and do nothing'.[58] For Machiavelli, imagining that the endurance of persecution led to renewal was just another aspect of the religion of idleness.

This historical digression reveals something that might otherwise be missed about Hirschman's reinterpretation of Machiavelli's *corruzione*. In his insistence that the latitude provided by slack might be beneficial, he is undermining Machiavelli's insistence that idleness and passivity were never the means through which renewal might be engendered, but rather the means through which both republics and religions come to ruin. And in allowing an ambivalence to slack, he is unconsciously reintroducing a duality that Christian apocalyptic thought encouraged, but which Machiavelli sought to exclude.[59] So, although Hirschman's slack is configured in the same terms as Machiavelli's corruption, it is not interpreted in the same way. Slack may be a form of corruption, but Hirschman reads it from a perspective that is closer to that of apocalyptic thought, for in his account slack is that form of decline which permits renewal.

Double time

All of this may seem rather remote from the concerns of the Eighteenth North American Wildlife Conference of 1953, and it is. Nevertheless, the sequence of parallels traced above may suggest something unexpected about the sort of political thinking represented by environmentalist policies of non-use or low growth.

If allowing environmental resources to remain idle is what Hirschman would have called slack, then any demand that nature should be preserved forever, or that its resources should be conserved for use by future generations, or that consumption should be reduced to limit environmental damage, is in effect a demand to introduce greater slack into both the economy and the environment. And if Hirschman's slack is a modern version of what Machiavelli would have called corruption, then advocating greater slack is tantamount to allowing the spread of corruption without any of the laws or pressure mechanisms needed to contain or reduce it.

In this context, it becomes easier to see why idle land is so often thought of in terms of human decadence.[60] When Edward P. Cliff, chief of the US Forest Service, stated in 1961 that 'nonproductive, misused and idle woodlands will add nothing to the economic and cultural foundation upon which our future as a nation and a civilization depend',[61] he was not just repeating the arguments of Gifford Pinchot, but rehearsing the republican argument against the corrupting effects of idleness that stretches back to Machiavelli – the idleness of trees just as much a menace to society as the idleness of men or other resources. Like those Christians who, according to Machiavelli, interpreted religion according to idleness, environmentalists are advocates of policies that are in themselves both forms of, and a stimulus to, economic decline and political decadence. Rather than warning of decline and disaster, environmentalists are in a sense advocating it.

However, unlike Machiavelli's corruption, the non-use or conservation of natural sources is, like slack, always double-edged. By wasting one set of opportunities it simultaneously creates others, and every loss can be counted as credit for the future. In this respect, environmental idleness resembles the more ambiguous transitions of apocalyptic thought, where periods of decay, tribulation and decadence are the means of change and renewal. If so, it may be necessary to reconsider the relationship of environmentalism to religion. It has long been suggested that ecological thought transposes ideas of sacredness from religion to nature.[62] And critics of the ecology movement have often located predictions of environmental degradation within the context of religious prophecies of doom.[63] On this reading, however, conservation, rather than being the preservation of the pristine or the primitive, is revealed as a form of decadence. And rather than being an eschatological mode of thought, focused on the proximity of the end, environmentalism emerges as apocalyptic in the sense that the decadence or dissolution of one order is recognized to be simultaneously constitutive of the new.

Joachim called overlaps between historical periods, in which more than one person of the Trinity was at work, 'double time'.[64] It is a concept that lends itself to wider application in the context of the 'tyranny of the contemporary' that so often stands in the way of thinking about the future.[65] Slack, of its very nature, seems to call for some form of double accounting across time, for its existence is not just the precondition of change, but actually constitutes both the opportunity and the means of renewal. As such, it posits the present as a form of double time in which the unused resources of today are simultaneously (not at some future time, but already) the resources of the future, the buffer that gives future generations the latitude needed to address their problems.

But thinking of conservation as a form of slack also carries more counterintuitive implications. It suggests that rather than treating environmental problems like climate change as pressure mechanisms galvanizing us into political mobilization and the creation of a taut green economy, it might be better to leave both natural and political resources unused, the better to deal with the uncertainties of the future. It is well known that the largest reductions in greenhouse emissions since 1990 are not the results of environmentally friendly policy, but the unintended consequence of economic decline in Eastern Europe after the fall of Communism. Perhaps economic decline and political inertia will turn out to be among the more useful instruments in the tool-kit we are assembling for the future.

7

Natural Cosmopolitanism

'Why can't we all live together?' That's a good question, and the problem simply stated is this: insofar as sociability comes naturally to us, it doesn't extend very far, yet blueprints for universal harmony are invariably abstractions that founder in the realities of everyday life. There does not seem to be such a thing as a natural cosmopolitanism, a form of universal sociability that is grounded in our biology and emerges spontaneously from it.

The problem is an ancient one. For Aristotle, it follows from the fact that man is a political animal that every city-state [polis] exists by nature. The continued existence of the human species depends on the union of men and women and the creation of families. When there are several related families, they constitute a village, which is the most basic form of society. And when several villages come together to form a community that is more or less self-sufficient, then we have the city-state, which has its origins in the necessities of life but continues for the sake of the good life. The city-state is therefore the creation of nature. If the more primitive forms of society are natural, the state must be too, for we consider what something is when fully developed to be its true nature, and the city-state is the final stage in the development of all those earlier social forms.[1]

Aristotle believes that the city-state is natural not only because it is the culmination of a biologically grounded process of formation, but because only in the social state is man able to make use of reason and speech, and it is only in society that he realizes his full potential. The proof that the city-state is naturally prior to the individual is that when separated from it the individual is less than self-sufficient. The individual must therefore be related to the state as a part to the whole. Someone who stands outside society altogether cannot really be human at all; if anything, they are more like an animal or a god.[2]

However, although every city may be natural, each is limited in size because 'it is perhaps impossible for a state with too large a population to have good legal government'. Since 'law is a form of order', good law requires good order, and as numbers increase it becomes progressively more difficult to maintain it. In the *Nicomachean Ethics* Aristotle indicates what he thinks that upper limit might be: '10 people would not make a city, but with 100,000 it is a city no longer.' Beyond that there comes a point at which order can be ensured only by a 'divine power'.[3]

If the city-state has a natural limit, what then happens outside it? Beyond the polis there is war. There are other Greeks, of course, with their own city-states, with whom wars may be fought only for the sake of peace, but most of those living beyond the borders of the state are barbarians, and barbarians, like animals, are a resource provided by nature to furnish what is necessary for life. The art of war will, therefore, 'by nature be in a manner an art of acquisition (for the art of hunting is a part of it) that is properly employed both against wild animals and against such of mankind as though designed by nature for subjection refuse to submit to it, inasmuch as warfare is by nature just'.[4]

According to Aristotle, nature therefore decrees a double movement: in one direction towards cooperation and communication, in the other towards acquisition and enslavement. Both are equally natural and the division between the two is to be found at the natural limits of the polis. The scope of Aristotle's political naturalism is therefore severely circumscribed: it is not just limited in extent but actually goes into reverse when that limit has been exceeded. Although not presented as such, Aristotle's political naturalism is communitarian rather than cosmopolitan in effect.

The cosmic city

Aristotle referred in passing to 'that greater city, the universe', but it was the Stoics who developed the idea.[5] Later Stoics differentiated 'two communities – the one, which is great and truly common, embracing gods and men, in which we look neither to this corner nor to that, but measure the boundaries of our state by the sun; the other, the one to which we have been assigned by the accident of our birth'.[6] The Stoics claimed that 'the universe is in the proper sense a city, but that those here on earth are not – they are called cities but are not really'.[7] From this perspective, Aristotle's polis is of the latter type, and would not qualify as a city at all.[8]

The idea of a cosmic city originated with Zeno, the founder of the Stoic school. According to Plutarch, Zeno maintained that 'our household arrangements should not be based on cities or parishes, each one marked out by its own legal system, but we should regard all men as our fellow-citizens and local residents, and there should be one way of life and order, like that of a herd grazing together and nurtured by a common law.'[9] What Zeno envisaged isn't altogether clear and has been the subject of much debate. Is the citizenry composed of all humans, or only of sages, or of sages and gods together, or of humans and gods, or all of the above? And how are they connected?[10]

The most common Stoic explanation for the naturalness of the cosmic city was (insofar as it can be reconstructed) *oikeiosis*. This is the noun from the verb *oikeioō*, to familiarize, and it refers both to the way 'nature familiarizes a human with him/herself', and the way 'nature familiarizes a human with other humans'.[11] Zeno's follower Chrysippus held that just as an animal's impulse to self-preservation leads to an awareness of its constitution and needs, so in the case of human beings the impulse to self-preservation leads to an awareness of reason and how to use it.[12]

The shift from Aristotle's idea of self-preservation through acquisition to a model of self-preservation through familiarization has significant implications. For the later Stoics, personal *oikeiosis* is just the prelude to social *oikeiosis*, the process through which human beings assimilate not just their physical but their social environment. The clearest account of this is provided much later by Cicero, for whom 'the general sociability of the human race' derives from parental love for their children: 'Hence it follows that mutual attraction between men is also something natural. Consequently, the mere fact that someone is a man makes it incumbent on another man not to regard him as alien.'[13]

It is this conception of *oikeiosis* that is brought together in Hierocles's famous description of expanding circles: 'Each one of us is as it were entirely encompassed by many circles, some smaller, others larger, the latter enclosing the former on the basis of their different and unequal dispositions relative to each other.' The individual mind is the centre, and the first circle encloses the body; the second, immediate family; the third, close relatives and so on until 'the outermost and largest circle, which encompasses all the rest, is that of the whole human race'.[14] What this seems to imply is that first of all one familiarizes oneself with one's own body, then the family, then the polis, then the *patria*, then the universe in one continuous movement. Man is still a political animal, but the implication of Stoic political naturalism is very different to Aristotle's: rather than turning back on itself at the borders of the city-state, human sociability leads inevitably on towards cosmopolitanism.

However, as Julia Annas points out, there is a problem here, because there appears to be no natural transition from personal to social *oikeiosis*: the partiality one feels for one's closest relatives cannot be extrapolated indefinitely to become a form of impartiality towards all other members of the human race: 'A demand of reason, that one treat all alike, is not the conclusion of a process of extending personal affections: that can result only in weak partiality, not in impartiality.'[15] As one ancient commentator pointed out, if the Stoics are saying that 'a man's appropriation to himself is equal to his appropriation in relation to the most distant Mysian ... That is contrary to plain fact and one's self-awareness'.[16]

However encompassing our sympathies, we can never become alienated from ourselves as we can from other people. We will always retain a preference for ourselves and those closest to us. Furthermore, the circles emanating from one centre will not necessarily align with those from another: your family, friends, neighbours and allies aren't going to be the same as mine, and our partiality is going to be distributed differently. And conflict will eventually arise, because when resources are scarce, 'we may grant the existence of philanthropy, but the situations of two shipwrecked sailors will refute them, where it is inevitable that only one of two survive'.[17] Just as Aristotle's city-states stand in a hostile relation to those beyond their borders and never make a transition from political naturalism to natural cosmopolitanism, so too *oikeiosis* can never extend far enough to give rise to the cosmic city of the Stoics' imagination without becoming mired in competition and conflict.

Although the Stoic city may be cosmic, it can never be cosmopolitan. In Zeno's account, 'only virtuous people in the Republic [are] citizens, friends, relatives, and free', while 'all who are not virtuous are personal and public enemies, slaves, and alienated from one another, including parents from children, brothers from brothers, relatives from relatives'.[18] As Arius Didymus later recorded, for the Stoic 'every fool is at enmity with the gods ... [but] friendship is harmony and concord'. On this view, what creates concord rather than conflict is the fact that all citizens have something in common, for concord is knowledge of common goods, and virtue, 'nurtured by a common law', and 'participation in reason, which is law by nature'.[19] But if this leaves all non-sages at war with each other, then for the Stoics cosmopolitanism is still just as much at odds with nature as it is in Aristotle, for the cosmic city precludes inclusivity.

Negative cosmopolitanism

This problem was perhaps built into the Stoic concept of the cosmic city from the outset, for the idea may have come from Heraclitus, for whom the common principle of the universe is war or strife. Chrysippus is said to have claimed that 'the universe of the wise is one, citizenship of it being held by gods and men together, and that war and Zeus are same, as Heraclitus also says'.[20] The idea to which Chrysippus refers is the fragment of Heraclitus that states: 'War is father of all and king of all.'[21] According to Aristotle, Heraclitus took exception to Homer's line, 'Would that Conflict might vanish from among gods and men' and insisted instead that 'war is shared and Conflict is justice, and that all things come to pass in accordance with conflict'. Or, as Heraclitus put it in a memorable phrase, 'The thunderbolt pilots all things.'[22]

If that is true, then whatever the starting point, a natural cosmopolitanism will always be impossible. However, there is another possibility, and it is one that can be glimpsed in

Heraclitus's enigmatic fragments on sleep. He, too, observes that although the *logos* is common, not everyone acknowledges it.[23] It is only the awake who share a common world; the asleep turn aside into private worlds.[24] If what is shared is war, and the waking world operates just as Homer says it does, and war 'is common and the killer gets killed', then it would seem to follow from this that the awake are at war, while the sleeper is not.[25] The only exception to the common world of war is therefore to be found in the private world of sleep, but that can access only the private world of dreams, and those, as Heraclitus emphasizes, are illusory: 'Death is all things we see awake; all we see asleep is sleep.'[26] Everything we see other than war must therefore be unreal.

Even if whatever sleepers experience is private and unreal, it is still perhaps something rather than nothing. There is a curious passage in Sextus Empiricus that fuses the Stoic conception of the rationality of the universe (which Heraclitus did not share) with what may be an authentic reflection of Heraclitus's account of sleep. In sleep, according to Sextus's account of Heraclitus, the intellect in us is separated from its connection to the common logos by which it becomes rational, and all that persists is a sort of root:

> In the same way, then, as coals when near to fire undergo an alteration and become fiery, but are put out when taken away from it, so too the portion of what encompasses us that dwells like a foreigner in our bodies becomes virtually devoid of reason in the case of separation, but in the case of natural connection through the multiple passages it becomes similar in kind to the whole.

And that, Sextus suggests, is why Heraclitus thinks that 'what appears in common to everyone is trustworthy ... whereas what strikes someone individually is untrustworthy'.[27]

The idea that the sleeper stands in the same relation to the common *logos* as an ember to a fire is an intriguing one, because of course Heraclitus identified what is common with fire and also with war. So if this passage were to be interpreted consistently in line with Heraclitus's other known views, it would suggest that being awake means being close to the fire, or being at war, while being asleep is like being an ember, or at peace. And this points to an extraordinary paradoxical conclusion that Heraclitus himself never drew. Perhaps peace is available not to those who participate in the *logos* but to those who do not; to the embers separated from the fire, the *alogoi*. If so, it would be the inverse of the Stoic version of the cosmic city in which those who share in the *logos* are friends and those who do not are enemies. Absurd? Not entirely.

That there is an alternative argument to be made here can be seen from the negative cosmopolitanism of the Cynics. Zeno's claim that 'all who are not virtuous are personal and political enemies' is the second of several 'disturbing theses' attributed to him by Diogenes Laertius.[28] These theses echo the antinomianism of the Cynics whose actions flouted the conventions of their own (and almost every other) society. The most notorious of them, Diogenes of Sinope, was said to live in a barrel and perform his bodily functions in public because he allowed convention 'no such authority as he allowed to natural right'.[29]

However, Diogenes claimed that someone living according to nature rather than according to convention or law might nevertheless still be counted a citizen. He was said to be 'citiless [*apolis*], homeless, deprived of country, a beggar, a wanderer, living life from day to day', but it was on this basis that he claimed to be 'a citizen of the universe' (*kosmopolitēs*, the origin of the word 'cosmopolitan').[30] Whereas Aristotle had claimed nature led to citizenship of the polis, the Cynics argued that it excluded it, but that being excluded from the polis nevertheless constituted a form of citizenship itself, because the only correct state was the one in the universe.[31]

What is the positive content of this claim? What form of citizenship does it entail? What is needed to maintain it and what would be needed to lose it? Clearly very little, save life itself. To be a citizen of the universe is merely to be alive in the universe. One does not have to be in contact with or even aware of the existence of the other citizens in order to be a citizen oneself. But one does have to co-exist, at least in the sense of not being dead, even if not awake or even human. Diogenes himself was said to have conversed with Alexander when half asleep, and to have identified as a dog: 'I fawn on those who give me anything, I yelp at those who refuse, and I set my teeth in rascals.'[32]

Being asleep and becoming animal are both ways of being *alogos*, of becoming an ember. According to Aristotle, it was the 'tribeless, lawless, hearthless one', 'the natural outcast' who was the lover of war. But here it is Diogenes, as tribeless, lawless and hearthless as anyone could be, who claims to be, not a lover of war, but the true citizen of the world.[33] And in a sense, Diogenes is right about this, because Aristotle's citizen can only ever be a citizen of the city-state, and thus in a state of war with those outside, so those who fail to be citizens of the polis are the only ones who can potentially be counted citizens of the universe.

All this means rethinking what might be involved in a natural cosmopolitanism. The initial assumption was that the quality of being natural was manifest through the natural growth and development of humans and other species. But there are two kinds of naturalism: the naturalness of growth and the naturalness of decay, and the Cynics embraced the latter. There was no need for temples and courts of law which might as well fall into disuse and ruin. Diogenes himself is reported to have defaced the currency. Like an ember withdrawn from the fire, a defaced coin returns to a state of latency. For the Cynic, the true cosmopolitan is someone who accepts and perhaps accelerates such entropic natural processes.

Kant

There is, then, a dilemma: either society can develop naturally in such a way that it can never be cosmopolitan, or there can be a form of cosmopolitanism that is natural enough but seems distinctly anti-social. No one seems to have tried to bring these strands together in antiquity. But they reappear in an essay by Kant, 'Idea for a Universal History from a Cosmopolitan Point of View', which tries to synthesize the two by arguing that they might actually work together.

Kant's first thesis is that 'All natural capacities of a creature are destined to evolve completely to their natural end.'[34]
Man's unique capacity is reason, which to develop fully
requires multiple lifetimes; therefore the natural capacities
of man are developed as a species and across time. This is
close to Aristotle, who claimed that 'man alone of all the
animals possesses speech [*logos*]' and that full development of this gift is only to be found in the city-state, which
demonstrates that 'man is more of a political animal than
bees or any other gregarious animals'.[35] However, whereas
for Aristotle the natural outcome of human nature is the
city-state, for Kant it is the cosmopolitan condition. Here,
according to Nussbaum, he takes up the Stoic vision of the
cosmic city and develops it into one where the 'community
of the peoples of the earth has developed so far that a vio-
lation of rights in one place is felt throughout the world,
[and] the idea of a law of world citizenship is no high-flown
or exaggerated notion'.[36]

Unlike the Stoics, Kant recognizes that there is no easy
passage from the expanding circles of concern to the cosmic city. What Kant offers instead is a novel argument that
encompasses not only Aristotle's political naturalism and
Stoic cosmopolitanism, but their seeming antithesis, an
(almost) Heraclitean insistence that war is a central and
ineradicable part of human life.[37] As he explains in another
essay, 'Perpetual Peace', war is nature's way of ensuring the
distribution of the human population across the surface of
the earth, and it 'requires no special motive but appears to
be engrafted on human nature'.[38] Indeed, as he elsewhere
observes: 'the maxim of violence in human beings and ...

their malevolent tendency to attack one another' is an a priori assumption when we talk about a state of nature.[39]

This assigns to war something like the role given to it by Heraclitus as the universal arbiter of human destinies. But for Kant, strife, rather than undermining all hope of cosmopolitanism, is the mechanism through which it is realized. On this argument, 'the means employed by Nature to bring about the development of all the capacities of men is their antagonism in society, so far as this is, in the end, the cause of a lawful order among men'. By antagonism in society, Kant means the 'unsocial sociability' i.e., the human tendency to both associate and compete ruthlessly for the benefits of association. Just as embers become red-hot as they approach the Heraclitean fire, so for Kant 'it is opposition that awakens all his powers, brings him to conquer his inclination to laziness'.[40]

The awakening not only effects the first steps from barbarism to culture; it is also the source of cosmopolitanism, 'the achievement of a universal civic society'. This happens through mutual constraint. In a now famous passage, Kant explains that

> need forces men, so enamoured otherwise of their boundless freedom, into [a] state of constraint. They are forced to it by the greatest of all needs, a need they themselves occasion inasmuch as their passions keep them from living long together in wild freedom. Once in such a preserve as a civic union, these same passions subsequently do the most good. It is just the same with trees in a forest: each needs the others, since each in seeking to take the air and sunlight from others must strive upward, and thereby each

realizes a beautiful, straight stature, while those that live in isolated freedom put out branches at random and grow stunted, crooked, and twisted.[41]

However, that is only the first step, for the internal constitution of the state cannot be perfected while the external relations between states remain hostile. Yet Kant is optimistic that this 'inevitable antagonism' will once again be 'used by Nature as a means to establish a condition of quiet and security'. Spurred by the continual ravages of war, nature eventually encourages states 'to step from the lawless condition of savages into a league of nations'.[42] Just as 'purposeless savagery held back the development of the capacities of our race' until it finally 'forced our race to renounce this condition and to enter into a civic order in which those capacities could be developed', so too the barbaric freedom of established states 'eventually gives rise to … a law of equilibrium and a united power to give it effect'. Thus, the natural condition of perpetual war results in its opposite: 'a cosmopolitan condition to secure the external safety of each state'.[43]

Kant appears to be synthesizing two traditions: one in which the *logos* is reason, as in the Stoics, and one in which the *logos* is war, as in Heraclitus. In this respect, his fable of the trees is reminiscent of Sextus's story about the fire and the coals. Here, however, height rather than heat has become the key variable, and there is now a temporal dimension: a tree becomes stunted when separated from the forest rather as the coal grows cold when away from the fire, but Kant's forest grows progressively taller over time, so a tree taken from the forest at t^2 will be taller than one left stranded at t^1 (whereas there is no implication that the fire becomes fiercer and that a coal taken from it will be hotter than the last one). The result is a secular theodicy in which war paradoxically becomes the means of realizing the telos of reason.

Why then is this not a satisfactory resolution of the problem posed at the start of the chapter, that of how there can be a political order that is both natural and cosmopolitan? Kant states that without this unsociable sociability, humans might never overcome their 'inclination to laziness' which would lead to

> an Arcadian shepherd's life, with all its concord, contentment, and mutual affection ... good-natured as the sheep they herd, [men] would hardly reach a higher worth than their beasts; they would not fill the empty place in creation by achieving their end, which is rational nature ... [and] all the excellent natural capacities of humanity would forever sleep, undeveloped.[44]

It is a picture that recalls Zeno's vision of a cosmic city in which all share 'one way of life and one order', like a herd feeding together. And yet for Kant it is this pastoral idyll that constitutes man's original sin: strife is needed to overcome idleness, just as lawful order is necessary to overcome the consequent war of all against all.

Nevertheless, the temptation to laziness remains, for even the cosmopolitan condition 'is not unattended by the danger that the vitality of mankind may fall asleep'. Nature wills that man 'should be plunged from sloth and passive contentment into labour and trouble, in order that he may find means of extricating himself from them'.[45] Yet the result of the cosmopolitan condition may be that 'sloth and passive contentment' set in once more. Why then should the race undergo what Kant describes as 'the cruellest hardships' only to arrive back at its starting point? With less sociability and less unsociability, man need never leave that condition in the first place. As Kant admits, 'Rousseau was not far wrong in preferring the state of savages, so long, that is, as the last stage to which the human race must climb is not attained.'[46]

According to Kant, all these hardships are necessary not for natural cosmopolitanism, which is only the means to an end, nor for the individual, who can never hope to benefit from them fully because one lifetime is not enough, but for the teleological fulfilment of the species, which is not to be cosmopolitan, but to be rational (just as in Aristotle). What Kant inadvertently shows is therefore that it is not human nature (which inclines towards laziness) but realizing the telos of humanity that is the cause of war. Without this goal there could indeed be an Arcadian herdlike existence. Kant also concedes that mankind might potentially lapse into this state at any point along the way, even at the half-way point of a cosmopolitan union of states. Without the need to stay awake out of fear, the human race will naturally go into torpor, like one of Heraclitus's coals withdrawn from the fire. So this life of concord might be possible not just at a primitive level but at more complex stages of social development as well, when the trees of the forest have already grown tall. Indeed, it would be the natural outcome of Kant's universal history, the inevitable consequence of peace, and the best guarantor of its perpetuity.

Division of labour

If the common waking world, the world formed by an active human sociability, is war, how can anything other than sleep bring peace? Although there can be no wakeful cosmopolitanism, sleep might allow a form of negative cosmopolitanism. Like the Cynic who has excluded himself from the polis to become a cosmopolitan unaware of others who might have done the same, the sleeper is in a sense the negative cosmopolitan par excellence. The sleeper is disengaged from the unsociable sociability of the common waking world, but potentially enjoys a sociable unsociability instead, not an antagonism that emerges from being in society, but a passive sociability that comes from being outside of it.

But in what sense can sleepers be said to be sociable? How, if sleepers are in private worlds, can they constitute any form of society, or have any form of sociability? It was a question that the Stoics had grappled with in their accounts of the cosmic city. Chrysippus argued that such a city assumed the possibility of friendship without acquaintance among sages who were unaware of each other's existence: 'If a single sage anywhere at all extends his finger prudently, all the sages through-out the inhabited world are benefited'.[47]

In this regard, Marcus Aurelius echoes the thinking of previous generations of Stoics on the cosmic city. However, following Heraclitus, he also allows for the possibility of a form of negative cosmopolitanism, and even for participation through sleep:

All of us are working together for the same end; some of us knowingly and purposefully, others unconsciously (as Heraclitus, I think, has remarked that 'even in their sleep men are at work' and contributing their share to the cosmic process). To one man falls this share of the task, to another that; indeed no small part is performed by that very malcontent who does all he can to hinder and undo the course of events.[48]

What Marcus seems to be doing here is using Heraclitus's saying about participatory sleep to address the Stoic vision of friendship at a distance and pose the question of the cosmic city in a new way. Rather than it being some common shared quality between sages that allows friendship among the unacquainted, it is the diversity and functional interaction of the separate parts, which is such that even a sleeper, who might appear to be making no contribution at all and be lost in an entirely private world, may be considered a participant. As Marcus emphasizes, we are born to work together 'like a man's two hands, feet, or eyelids, or like the upper and lower rows of his teeth. To obstruct each other is against Nature's law'.[49]

It is a vision of sociability that perhaps resonates in modernity more than ever before. Marcus's claim that even the malcontent plays their part is echoed in Mandeville's dictum that 'The worst of all the Multitude / Did something for the Common Good'.[50] But this involves a different vision of sociability to that of the cosmic city as a herd of cows or flock of sheep. It is perhaps best illustrated by Durkheim, who picks up Darwin's point that there is less conflict the more species differ and the less they have to do with each other:

> What is advantageous to one is without value to the others. The chances of conflict thus diminish with chances of meeting, and the more so as the species or varieties are more distant from one another ... Animals themselves, prosper more when they differ more. On an oak-tree there were found two hundred species of insects having no other relationship than neighbourhood ... Men submit to the same law. In the same city, 'different occupations can co-exist without being obliged mutually to destroy one another, for they pursue different objects.' ... Since they perform different services, they can perform them parallelly.[51]

Rather than being like a herd grazing on a common pasture, this is a version of the cosmic city in which each individual or species is in its private realm, like someone asleep. But more than that, sleep prefigures the division of labour. Asleep, each benefits the others by not being at war with them, yet no contact is needed for this benefit to accrue, and both parties are oblivious to it. Sleep is in this respect an intimation of modernity. A complex society in which everyone depends on everyone else is a world of at least semi-oblivious mutual dependency, like a world of unihemispheric sleepers.

It is Arendt who makes this connection explicit: 'the political realm [that] rises directly out of acting together, the "sharing of words and deeds"' does not always exist, because 'although all men are capable of deed and word, most do not live in it'.[52] At the same time, 'to be deprived of it means to be deprived of reality' and without the reality guaranteed by the presence of others, everything 'comes and passes away like a dream'. It is, Arendt notes, just as Heraclitus said: 'the world is one and common to those who are awake, but everybody who is asleep turns away to his own'.[53] So modern mass society, where 'the world between [people] has lost its power to gather them together, to relate and to separate them', has become like a world of sleepers each lost in their private dreams. With 'the emergence of society' the private has become an unworthy substitute for the public, rather as when Diogenes performed private acts in public.[54] Instead of the world that gathered people together there is only the void that Arendt calls 'the social'.

The necessity of sleep

If the social describes a situation in which everyone might as well be asleep because their collective intentions amount to nothing, then it is this, ironically, that emerges as perhaps the most promising form of natural cosmopolitanism. Aristotle's naturalism does not extend beyond the self-sufficient polis, and Stoic *oikeiosis* leads to a cosmic city only through exclusion. The only viable form of cosmopolitanism therefore appears to be the negative kind exemplified by Diogenes, where exclusion from a shared public realm is the condition of universalism. That might appear to be possible only at the primitive level of existence exemplified by Diogenes himself. But as Kant emphasizes, the natural inclination to laziness never goes away, and without fear to keep them awake human beings will always quickly fall asleep once more. In modernity, the division of labour allows that to happen more easily than ever before, and the result is potentially a worldless cosmopolitanism, the outcome not of the growth of a shared world to cosmic dimensions, but of the decay of the public realm as it becomes more complex and cosmopolitan. If every city exists by nature, the cosmic city exists by nature, asleep.

This is not, or not just, a metaphor. Human beings are generally asleep for about eight hours a day, so about one-third of the lifetime encompassed by any political arrangement is sleeping time. Sleep is therefore an important part of what has to be accounted for in every political theory. Indeed, the fact that people fall asleep is itself significant, because it is what gives rise to the originary division of labour in which constant individual vigilance gives way to alliances between people. Because a sleeper is always vulnerable to attack, peace is necessary for sleep, and so sleep entails not just being peaceful but also being at peace. It follows from this that the more sleepers there are and the longer they sleep, the more likely it is that peace will reign, for sleepers are both pacific and at peace. Mammals usually sleep more the less they have to fear.

Every political theory must presuppose that someone is asleep and allow for the possibility that there are times when everyone might be. A theory that was inapplicable to such an eventuality would not be a political theory about human beings at all, but rather about time-slices of human life. It would be premissed on waking people up, or on artificially keeping them awake, because it would become redundant the minute they fell asleep. And that is why, as Jonathan Crary has argued, capitalism has reduced sleeping time from ten to six and a half hours in little over a century as 'the planet becomes re-imagined as a non-stop work site or an always open shopping mall'.[55]

If sleep has emerged as the last remaining obstacle to the triumph of capitalism, that is because it has always been the enemy of every kind of war, whether war is assumed to be an inexorable destiny (as in Heraclitus and Carl Schmitt) or merely the pressure mechanism needed for human progress (as in Machiavelli and Kant). The alternative it offers is not just physical rest, but a society that enables us to sleep, and potentially allows us all to sleep at the same time, without demanding that we wake up before we're ready to do so; a society in which the human condition converges with sleep to the degree that everyone could be asleep without it making any difference. And that is not impossible. The reason that we can't all live together is that we are awake. But sleep comes naturally.

Notes

1 The Concept of the Social

1   A. A. Long and D. N. Sedley eds, *The Hellenistic Philosophers* [hereafter THP], vol. 1, Cambridge 1987, pp. 15 (1F) and 13 (1A).

2   See Michael Frede, 'The Skeptic's Two Kinds of Assent and the Question of the Possibility of Knowledge' in *Essays in Ancient Philosophy*, Minneapolis 1987, pp. 20–22 and M. F. Burnyeat, 'Can the Sceptic Live His Scepticism?' in *Explorations in Ancient and Modern Philosophy*, Cambridge 2012, pp. 205–35.

3   Diogenes Laertius in THP, p. 14 (1C).

4   THP, p. 468 (71A).

5   See Katja Maria Vogt, 'Scepticism and Action' in R. Bett ed., *The Cambridge Companion to Ancient Scepticism*, New York 2010, pp. 165–180.

6   David Hume, *Enquiries Concerning Human Understanding*, 3rd ed., Oxford 1975, pp. 160 and 158–9.

7   David Hume, *A Treatise on Human Nature*, Oxford 1978, p. 657 (Abstract) and p. 183 (T1.4.1).

8   Ibid., p. 415 (T2.3.3).

9   Bernard Williams, *Moral Luck*, Cambridge 1981, pp. 101–13.

10 John R. Searle, *Rationality in Action*, Cambridge, MA 2001, pp. 27–8.

11 John R. Searle, *The Construction of Social Reality* [hereafter CSR], London 1995, p. 122. See also his *Making the Social World* [hereafter

MSW], New York 2010, p. 10. These two books contain clear and comprehensive accounts of Searle's social ontology, and the exposition that follows draws heavily on both. There is considerable overlap between the two, but there are also differences, as explained in MSW, pp. 11–15 and 19–24. The chief innovation of MSW is the insistence on the need for Status Function Declarations in the creation of institutional facts. This emphasis is not reflected in what follows, for it does nothing to strengthen Searle's case against the criticisms advanced here.

12 Strabo quoting Megasthenes, cited in Christopher J. Beckwith, *Greek Buddha*, Princeton 2015, p. 73.

13 F. Nietzsche, *Will to Power*, tr. W. Kaufmann and R. J. Hollingdale, New York 1967, p. 451 (§ 853).

14 Hannah Arendt, *The Human Condition* [hereafter HC], Chicago 1958, pp. 22, 52, and 173.

15 Ibid., pp. 183 and 197 (cf. Aristotle, *Nicomachean Ethics*, tr Harris Rackham, Cambridge, MA 1926, 1126b12).

16 Hannah Arendt, *On Revolution*, Harmondsworth 1973, p. 175.

17 HC, p. 237.

18 Ibid., p. 53. On 'the social' in Arendt see Hannah Fenichel Pitkin, *The Attack of the Blob*, Berkeley 1998.

19 HC, p. 208.

20 Ibid., p. 28.

21 Émile Durkheim, *The Division of Labour in Society*, tr W. D. Halls, Basingstoke 1984, pp. xxxiv–v and 304–5.

22 Ibid., p. xxxv; HC, p. 204.

23 CSR, pp. 6–7 and 41.

24 MSW, p. 27. On collective intention in animals see further Robert A. Wilson, 'Collective Intentionality in Non-Human Animals' in Marija Jankovic and Kirk Ludwig, eds, *Routledge Handbook of Collective Intentionality*, New York 2017, pp. 420–32.

25 CSR, p. 23.

26 MSW, pp. 47–8.

27 Ibid., p. 59.

28 CSR, p. 28; MSW, p. 96. In MSW Searle adds the requirement that the creation of an institutional fact requires a 'standing Declaration' of a constitutive rule to the effect that 'X counts as Y in C' (p. 13).

29   CSR, pp. 27–8 and 48.

30   Ibid., pp. 119 and 117.

31   MSW, pp. 8–9.

32   CSR, p. 94; MSW, p. 142.

33   MSW, p. 82.

34   CSR, p. 117.

35   MSW, p. 166.

36   In CSR, pp. 96–7, Searle acknowledges that honorary functions do not carry deontic powers, but in MSW, p. 24, he claims that even an honorary status function bring some deontic powers (though presumably rather less than those of their substantive equivalents).

37   MSW, pp. 57–8 allows that collective intention can be reduced to I-intention plus mutual belief, or acceptance or recognition, or even indifference or apathy.

38   Ibid., p. 94.

39   Francesco Guala, *Understanding Institutions*, Princeton 2016, pp. 57–68.

40   Francesco Guala and Frank Hindriks, 'A Unified Social Ontology', *The Philosophical Quarterly* 65, 2015, p. 189 and 179; CSR, p. 71.

41   Ibid., p. 189.

42   BBC.com, 'Czech Deer Still Avoid Iron Curtain', 23 April 2014.

43   See Searle CSR, pp. 144–5.

44   CSR, p. 71.

45   Brian Epstein, *The Ant Trap*, New York 2015, pp. 51–3 and 74–87.

46   See Brian Epstein, 'How Many Kinds of Glue Hold the Social World Together?' in Mattia Galloti and John Michael, eds, *Social Ontology and Social Cognition*, Dordrecht 2014, pp. 41–55.

47   MSW, pp. 156 and 116–17.

48   On Searle and Durkheim see Steven Lukes, 'Searle versus Durkheim' in S. L. Tsohatzidis ed., *Intentional Acts and Institutional Facts: Essays on John Searle's Social Ontology*, Dordrecht 2007, pp. 203–17.

49   Otto Neurath quoted in H. Rutte, 'The Philosopher Neurath' in T. E. Uebel, *Rediscovering the Forgotten Vienna Circle*, Dordrecht 1991, p. 94n.

50   John Rawls, *Political Liberalism*, New York 1993, p. 150.

51   Brian Barry, *Justice as Impartiality*, Oxford 1995, 168–173. However, Barry claims that 'from scepticism alone nothing follows in the way of political principles, including the principle of neutrality' (p. 172).

52 W. Quine, *From a Logical Point of View*, Cambridge, MA 1980, pp. 1–19.

53 MSW, p. 82.

54 Elliott Sober, *Ockham's Razors: A User's Manual*, Cambridge 2015, p. 150.

55 Bruno Latour, *On the Modern Cult of the Factish Gods*, Durham, NC 2010, pp. 25–7.

56 THP, p. 15 (1F).

57 Sextus Empiricus, *Outlines of Scepticism*, tr. J. Annas and J. Barnes, Cambridge 2000, pp. 3 and 7.

58 Frede, 'The Skeptic's Two Kinds', pp. 208–9.

59 MSW, p. 57.

60 THP, p. 450 (69A). (See Vogt, 'Scepticism', pp. 167ff.)

61 Frede, 'The Skeptic's Two Kinds', p. 208.

62 Vogt, 'Scepticism', p. 171.

63 CSR, p. 95.

64 Guala, *Understanding*, p. 66.

65 MSW, p. 201.

66 On reification see Andrew Feenberg, especially 'Lukács's Theory of Reification and Contemporary Social Movements', *Rethinking Marxism* 27, 2015, pp. 490–507.

67 Georg Lukács, *History and Class Consciousness*, tr R. Livingstone, London 1971, pp. 83 and 184.

68 Michael J. Thompson, 'Collective Intentionality, Social Domination, and Reification', *Journal of Social Ontology* 3, 2017, pp. 218 and 225.

69 Karl Marx, *Capital*, tr. S. Moore and E. Aveling, vol. 1, New York 1906, p. 83.

70 Lukács, *History*, p. 169.

71 Ibid., pp. 177 and 184.

72 Bertell Ollman, 'Marx's Vision of Communism', *Critique* 8, 1977, p. 38.

73 Karl Marx, *Early Writings*, tr. R. Livingstone and G. Benton, London 1975, p. 348.

74 Ibid., p. 366; Alasdair MacIntyre, *Marxism*, London 1953, p. 23.

75 According to Imre Lakatos's biographer, János Radványi, Lukács was aware that his argument *History and Class Consciousness* was related to scepticism, even if he was never explicit about his use of 'Pyrrhonism's dialectical acids'. John Kadvany, 'The Extraterritoriality of Imre

Lakatos: A Conversation with János Radványi' in George E. Marcus, *Paranoia Within Reason*, Chicago 1999, pp. 51–2.

76 Herbert Marcuse, *Reason and Revolution*, 2nd ed., London 2000, p. 112ff. See also Lucio Colletti's critique in *Marxism and Hegel*, tr L. Garner, London 1973, pp. 68–85.

77 John R. Searle, *The Rediscovery of the Mind*, Cambridge, MA 1992, p. 190; John R. Searle, *Consciousness and Language*, Cambridge 2002, p. 264; John R. Searle, *Intentionality*, Cambridge 1983, 154.

78 CSR, p. 143.

79 Ibid., pp. 5 and 143–6.

80 Searle, *Intentionality*, p. 150.

81 Adapted from CSR, pp. 141–2.

82 Searle, *Consciousness*, p. 154.

83 MSW, p. 156.

84 Ibid., p. 154. See also Enrico Terrone and Daniela Tagliafico, 'Normativity of the Background: A Contextualist Account of Social Facts' in M. Gallotti and J. Michael, eds, *Perspectives on Social Ontology and Social Cognition*, Dordrecht 2014, pp. 69–86.

85 CSR, p. 147.

86 HC, pp. 321 and 118.

87 Nietzsche, *Will to Power*, p. 241 (§ 437).

88 THP, p. 13 (1B) and Richard Bett, *Pyrrho, his Antecedents, and his Legacy*, Oxford 2000, p. 162n.

89 Sextus, *Outlines*, p. 4 (1.8).

90 MSW, pp. 151–2 and 164. See also John R. Searle, *Freedom and Neurobiology*, New York 2007, pp. 79–109.

91 Åsa Andersson, *Power and Social Ontology*, Malmö 2007, p. 151.

92 CSR, p. 19.

93 See Frank Hindriks, 'How Social Objects (Fail to) Function', *Journal of Social Philosophy* 53, 2020, pp. 483–99.

94 CSR, pp. 144–5.

95 See Thorvald Gran, 'John Searle on the Concept of Political Power', *Journal of Institutional Economics* 8, 2012, pp. 71–91.

96 MSW, p. 163.

97 Ibid., pp. 157–60.

98 Sextus, *Outlines*, pp. 4 and 5 (1.8 and 10).

99 John Bellamy Foster argues that the importance of Marx's ecological value analysis 'lies precisely in the fact that it traces capitalism's fundamental contradiction to the alienation of nature and the alienation of human production, as two sides of a single contradiction', see 'Marx's Ecological Value Analysis', *Monthly Review* 52:4, 2000, pp. 39–47.

100 Jason. W. Moore, *Capitalism in the Web of Life*, London 2015, pp. 169–92.

101 Forest Rohwer, quoted in Alan Weisman, *The World Without Us*, London 2007, p. 274.

102 Durkheim, *Division*, p. 213.

2 Vectors of the Biopolitical

1 Michel Foucault, *The History of Sexuality: An Introduction*, tr Robert Hurley, Harmondsworth 1984, pp. 143, 142.

2 Foucault, *History of Sexuality*, p. 139.

3 Foucault quoted in Giorgio Agamben, *Homo Sacer: Sovereign Power and Bare Life*, tr Daniel Heller-Roazen, Stanford 1998, p. 3; henceforth HS.

4 'The chief characteristic of this specifically human life ... is that it is itself always full of events which ultimately can be told as a story, establish a biography; it is of this life, *bios* as distinguished from mere ζōē, that Aristotle said that it "somehow is a kind of *praxis*".' Hannah Arendt, *The Human Condition* [1958], Chicago 1998, p. 97; henceforth HC.

5 HS, p. 1.

6 Aristotle, *Politics*, tr Harris Rackham, Cambridge, MA 1932, 1252b30.

7 HS, p. 2.

8 Ibid., pp. 8, 4, 6.

9 Ibid., p. 6.

10 Ibid., pp. 181, 8.

11 Giorgio Agamben, *The Open: Man and Animal*, tr Kevin Attell, Stanford 2004, pp. 34–8. In this respect, Agamben argues, modernity differs from antiquity, which tended to humanize the animal, treating the slave, the barbarian and the foreigner as 'figures of an animal in human form'.

12 HS, p. 183.

13 Ibid., p. 105.

14 Ibid., pp. 9 and 111.

15 Amartya Sen, 'Plural Utility', *Proceedings of the Aristotelian Society* 81, 1980/1, pp. 193–215.

16 Amartya Sen, 'Well-Being, Agency and Freedom', *Journal of Philosophy* 82, 1985, pp. 169–221.

17 Amartya Sen, *On Ethics and Economics*, Oxford 1987, p. 64 fn. and Aristotle, *Nicomachean Ethics*, 1097b28.

18 Martha Nussbaum, 'Nature, Function and Capability: Aristotle on Political Distribution', *Oxford Studies in Ancient Philosophy* 6, 1988, suppl. vol., p. 146 (citing Aristotle, *Politics*, 1324a23–5).

19 Martha Nussbaum, 'Non-Relative Virtues: An Aristotelian Approach' in Nussbaum and Amartya Sen, eds, *The Quality of Life*, Oxford 1993, p. 265.

20 Aristotle, *Nic. Ethics*, 1097b33–1098a4 (translation modified). Aristotle later explains that reason (*logos*) includes 'activity of the soul in accordance with reason or not without reason', a definition that might just include slaves and barbarians. It is interesting to note (in the light of Agamben's claims to the contrary) that, although the word is not actually repeated, *zōē* is here used to describe each of the three kinds of life, including the *praktikē zōē*. Nussbaum notes that 'if one comprehensively surveys the evidence, one discovers that *zōē* and *bios* function in exactly the same way: when they are used of a type or manner of life, they always designate a total mode or way of life, organized around the item named'. Martha Nussbaum, 'Aristotle on Human Nature and the Foundations of Ethics' in James Altham and Ross Harrison, eds, *World, Mind and Ethics: Essays on the Ethical Philosophy of Bernard Williams*, Cambridge 1995, p. 116; see pp. 128–9, fn. 50 for examples.

21 Martha Nussbaum, 'Human Capabilities, Female Human Beings' in Nussbaum and Jonathan Glover, eds, *Women, Culture and Development: A Study of Human Capabilities*, Oxford 1995, p. 81.

22 Nussbaum, 'Nature, Function', p. 146; and 'Human Nature', p. 103.

23 Martha Nussbaum, *Frontiers of Justice: Disability, Nationality, Species Membership*, Cambridge, MA 2006, pp. 105, 1; henceforth FJ.

24 FJ, pp. 176 and 87, see also p. 158.

25 Ibid., 130–2.

26 Ibid., p. 188.

27 Ibid., pp. 366, 388, 390, 370–1.

28 Aristotle, *Nic. Ethics*, 1095b20.

29 FJ, p. 347; Agamben, *The Open*, p. 47.

30 Aristotle, *Politics*, 1253a.

31 Aristotle, *Historia Animalium*, 1488a10.

32 HS, p. 106.

33 Ibid., p. 187.

34 Ibid., p. 90.

35 Rousseau, *Emile*, book 4; epigraph for Nussbaum, 'Human Capabilities, Female Human Beings', p. 63.

36 See David Depew, 'Humans and Other Political Animals in Aristotle's *History of Animals*', *Phronesis* 40, 1995, pp. 156–81.

37 Aristotle, *Politics*, 1254b22–3, 1260a10–14.

38 Ibid., 1252b12.

39 Aristotle, *Eudemian Ethics*, 1242a23.

40 HS, pp. 37–8.

41 HC, p. 46.

42 Ibid., pp. 97, 22.

43 Ibid., pp. 176, 118.

44 Ibid., pp. 52, 7, 2.

45 Ibid., pp. 126, 320–1.

46 Ibid., pp. 67, 330, 69.

47 Ibid., pp. 44–5.

48 Ibid., pp. 72–3.

49 FJ, p. 85. Before Nussbaum turned her attention to Aristotle, Marx was Sen's chief point of reference; see Sen, 'Plural Utility', p. 198; 'Well-being', p. 202 fn.; *On Ethics*, p. 46 fn.

50 FJ, pp. 74–5.

51 Marx, 'Economic and Philosophical Manuscripts', quoted in Nussbaum, 'Nature, Function', p. 145.

52 Nussbaum, 'Nature, Function', p. 183.

53 HC, p. 254.

54 Agamben, *The Open*, p. 9.

55 Karl Marx, 'Economic and Philosophical Manuscripts', *Early Texts*, tr David McLellan, Oxford 1971, p. 148.

56 Agamben, *The Open*, p. 76.

57 Marx, Introduction, *Grundrisse*, tr Martin Nicolaus, Harmondsworth 1973, p. 84.

58   Marx, 'Economic and Philosophical Manuscripts', *Early Texts*, p. 140.

59   Ibid., p. 149.

60   Marx, 'On the Jewish Question', *Early Writings*, tr Thomas Bottomore, London 1963, p. 31; and 'Economic and Philosophical Manuscripts', *Early Texts*, p. 150.

61   Marx, 'On the Jewish Question', *Early Writings*, p. 31.

62   Marx, 'Economic and Philosophical Manuscripts', *Early Writings*, pp. 160–1.

3 The Limits of Multitude

1   Michael Hardt and Antonio Negri, *Multitude*, London 2004, pp. 99, 106.

2   Ibid., p. 103.

3   Paolo Virno, *A Grammar of the Multitude*, New York 2004, pp. 21, 23.

4   Antonio Negri, *The Savage Anomaly*, Minneapolis 1991, p. 19; Etienne Balibar, *Masses, Classes, Ideas*, London 1994, p. 16; Virno, *Grammar*, p. 22. See also Warren Montag, *Bodies, Masses, Power*, London 1999 and Negri, *Subversive Spinoza*, Manchester 2005; Balibar's *Spinoza and Politics*, London 1998, provides a more balanced account.

5   Virno, *Grammar*, p. 23.

6   *Multitude*, pp. 242–3.

7   Negri, *Savage Anomaly*, p. 199; Montag, *Bodies*, p. 92.

8   Balibar, *Masses*, p. 17.

9   Virno, *Grammar*, p. 21.

10   *Multitude*, p. 340 and Montag, *Bodies*, pp. 84–5.

11   Hobbes, *The Elements of Law, Natural and Politic [1650]* 21.11, ed. J. C. A. Gaskin, Oxford 1994.

12   Hobbes, *De Cive [1642]*, 6.1. All quotations from *De Cive* are from the edition translated and edited by Richard Tuck and Michael Silverthorne as *On the Citizen*, Cambridge 1998; I have consistently substituted 'multitude' for 'crowd' as the translation of *multitudo*.

13   *Elements*, 21.11 and *De Cive*, 6.1.

14   *De Cive*, 6.1.

15   Ibid., 12.8.

16   Ibid., 6.1.

17   Hobbes, *Leviathan [1651]*, ed. Richard Tuck, Cambridge 1991, p 114.

18 *De Cive*, 7.11.

19 Ibid., 12.8.

20 Ibid., 13.13.

21 Ibid., 7.5.

22 *Elements*, 27.4.

23 Cicero, *The Republic*, 1.39.

24 Augustine, *City of God*, 19.21.

25 Ibid., 19.24.

26 Augustine, *Sermo* 103, quoted in J. D. Adams, *The 'Populus' of Augustine and Jerome: A Study in the Patristic Sense of Community*, New Haven 1971, p. 35.

27 See M. S. Kempshall, *'De re publica* 1.39 in Medieval and Renaissance Political Thought'* in J. G. F. Powell and J. A. North, eds, *Cicero's Republic*, London 2001, pp. 99–135.

28 Aristotle, *Politics*, 1279a, tr Benjamin Jowett, Oxford 1905; Thomas Aquinas, *In libros politicorum Aristotelis expositio*, ed. Raimondo Spiazzi, Rome 1951, p. 139.

29 Marsilius of Padua, *Defensor Pacis [1324]*, 1.12.5, tr Alan Gewirth, New York 1956.

30 Spinoza, *Theologico-Political Treatise [1670]*, tr R. H. M. Elwes, New York 1951, p. 205; henceforward TTP.

31 Spinoza, *Political Treatise [1677]*, 3.7, tr R. H. M. Elwes, New York 1951; henceforward TP. Balibar reviews interpretations of this phrase (which first appears at TP 3.2) in 'Potentia multitudinis, quae una veluti mente ducitur' in Marcel Senn and Manfred Walther, eds, *Ethik, Recht und Politik bei Spinoza*, Zürich 2001, pp. 105–37.

32 TP, 2.16.

33 Ibid., 2.13.

34 Ibid., 2.15.

35 Aristotle, *Politics*, 1253a.

36 TP, 3.2.

37 Ibid., 8.19.

38 Ibid., 3.7.

39 Ibid., 2.21.

40 Spinoza, *Letters*, tr. Samuel Shirley, Indianapolis 1995, p. 192.

41 Spinoza, *Ethics [1677]*, 4.P32 and 4.P35, tr Edwin Curley, London 1996.

42　TP, 1.5.

43　TTP, p. 216.

44　TP, 6.1.

45　Aquinas, *In libros politicorum*, p. 151. Aquinas's commentary (which his pupil Peter of Auvergne takes up at the end of 3.6) was routinely published with Latin translations of the *Politics* well into the seventeenth century (e.g., the Paris edition of 1645). It is quite likely that Spinoza, who read Aristotle in Latin, was acquainted with the *Politics* through such an edition.

46　Aristotle, *Politics*, 1286a and 1282a. For a contemporary discussion of this phenomenon, see James Surowiecki, *The Wisdom of Crowds*, London 2004.

47　Aristotle, *Politics*, 1281a–b.

48　TTP, p. 206.

49　TP, 8.3.

50　Ibid., 9.14.

51　*Elements*, 19.5.

52　*De Cive*, 5.5.

53　Ibid., 5.4.

54　*Leviathan*, p. 119.

55　*Ethics*, 4.P18.S, and 4.P35.C2.

56　Ibid., 4.P18.S; cf. Aristotle, *Politics*, 1281a.

57　*Ethics*, 4.P35.

58　Bernard Mandeville, *The Fable of the Bees [1714]*, Oxford 1924, vol. 1, p. 347.

59　Mandeville, *Fable*, vol. 2, p. 132; vol. 1, p. 344.

60　Mandeville, *Fable*, vol. I, pp. 124, 346–7.

61　Smith, *The Theory of Moral Sentiments [1759]*, London 1976, pp. 184–5.

62　Smith, *The Wealth of Nations [1776]*, Book 4, chapter 2.

63　Dugald Stewart, *Collected Works*, vol. 2, Edinburgh 1854, p. 248.

64　Rousseau, *The Social Contract*, 2.1 and 2.3.

65　*Multitude*, p. 329.

66　Ibid., pp. 242, 338.

67　Ibid., pp. 91–3.

68　Ibid., p. 339.

69　Virno, *Grammar*, p. 42.

70   Marx, *Grundrisse*, London 1973, p. 706.

71   Virno, *Grammar*, pp. 64, 66.

72   Friedrich Hayek, *Studies in Philosophy, Politics and Economics*, London 1967, p. 73.

73   *Multitude*, p. 337.

74   Hayek, *The Constitution of Liberty*, London 1960, p. 26; Virno, *Grammar*, p. 106.

75   *Multitude*, p. 197.

4 States of Failure

1   G. W. F. Hegel, *Philosophy of Right*, tr T. M. Knox, Oxford 1952, §258; hereafter PR. I follow Knox's 1952 translation throughout, apart from the citation referenced in footnote 5 below, where I use H. B. Nisbet's.

2   See Norbert Waszek, *The Scottish Enlightenment and Hegel's Account of Civil Society*, Dordrecht 1988, and Mark Neocleous, 'From Civil Society to the Social', *British Journal of Sociology* 46, 1995, pp. 395– 408.

3   PR, §183.

4   Hegel, *Elements of the Philosophy of Right*, tr H. B. Nisbet, Cambridge 1991, §182.

5   PR, §186.

6   Ibid., §199.

7   Ibid., §184A.

8   Ibid., §182A, 187.

9   Ibid., §260.

10 Ibid., §268.

11 Ibid., §258.

12 Ibid., §199.

13 L. T. Hobhouse, *The Metaphysical Theory of the State*, London 1918, p. 6.

14 Bernard Bosanquet, *The Philosophical Theory of the State*, 4th ed., London 1965, pp. 151, 150.

15 Hobhouse, *Metaphysical Theory*, pp. 43, 81.

16 Ibid., p. 82.

17 See Domenico Losurdo, *La catastrofe della Germania e l'immagine di Hegel*, Milan 1987, pp. 105–49.

18 Carl Schmitt, *The Concept of the Political*, tr G. Schwab, Chicago 1996,

pp. 29–30, 33; see also Jean-François Kervégan, *Hegel, Carl Schmitt, le politique entre spéculation et positivité*, Paris 1992.

19   Schmitt, *Concept*, pp. 22, 72, 57.

20   PR, §258.

21   Ibid., §181, 185.

22   Engels quoted in Lenin, *The State and Revolution*, tr R. Service, London 1992, p. 16.

23   Ibid., p. 80.

24   Antonio Gramsci, *Selections from the Prison Notebooks*, tr Q. Hoare, London 1971, p. 263.

25   Ibid., p. 253.

26   See Cécile Laborde, *Pluralist Thought and the State in Britain and France, 1900–25*, Basingstoke 2000, and David Runciman, *Pluralism and the Personality of the State*, Cambridge 1997.

27   Carl Schmitt, 'Ethic of State and Pluralist State' in Chantal Mouffe, *The Challenge of Carl Schmitt*, London 1999, pp. 195–6.

28   Carl Schmitt, *The Leviathan in the State Theory of Thomas Hobbes*, tr G. Schwab, Westport 1996, p. 74.

29   Maxime Leroy quoted in Laborde, *Pluralist Thought*, p. 32.

30   J. N. Figgis quoted in Laborde, *Pluralist Thought*, p. 47.

31   J. N. Figgis, *Antichrist, and other Sermons*, London 1913, p. 266.

32   PR, §251, 256.

33   Ibid., §303.

34   Ibid., §290A and 303.

35   Jean-Paul Sartre, *Critique of Dialectical Reason*, vol. 1, tr A. Sheridan-Smith, London 2004, pp. 348, 284–5; hereafter CDR.

36   CDR, p. 349.

37   Ibid., p. 634.

38   Ibid., pp. 370, 357.

39   Ibid., p. 65.

40   Ibid., p. 591. The process can be tracked through the shifting role of what Sartre calls 'the third' (the third party, or object, whose presence unifies the group). When merely a gathering, like the bus queue, 'the third party is submerged in seriality, being structured *a priori* as the Other, and therefore as Other than everyone and Other than us', p. 366. In the group-in-fusion, the third party is interiorized within the group as

each becomes a third to the reciprocities of the others, but 'the counterpart of the integration of each third party into the group is ... reciprocal exile' (p. 585), for in regulating the reciprocities of others each is constituted as a 'quasi- sovereign', an excluded third party. The entropy of the group is a function of the increasing alterity of 'the third'.

41 See G. Brennan and P. Pettit, 'Hands Invisible and Intangible', *Synthese* 94, 1993, pp. 191–225.

42 CDR, p. 662.

43 See I. Prigogine and I. Stengers, *Order Out of Chaos*, London 1984. The standard example is the Bénard cell – a hexagonal convection cell that appears at a certain point when a vertical temperature gradient is applied to a horizontal liquid layer.

44 Schmitt, *Concept*, p. 53.

45 Carl Schmitt, 'The New *Nomos* of the Earth' in *The* Nomos *of the Earth*, tr G. L. Ulmen, New York 2003, p. 354.

46 Schmitt, *The* Nomos, p. 247.

47 Samuel Huntington, *The Clash of Civilizations*, London 1996, p. 82.

48 Francis Fukuyama, *The End of History and the Last Man*, London 1992.

49 Alexandre Kojève, *Outline of a Phenomenology of Right*, tr. B-P. Frost and R. Howse, Lanham, MD 2000, p. 324 and p. 141, n. 28. Like Sartre, Kojève expresses this in terms of a relationship of thirds. In the universal and homogeneous state the third, who decides disputes between two parties, can be anyone at all: he or she does not have to belong to one state as opposed to another, nor to an exclusive group. So each is both sovereign to all (like Sartre's group-in-fusion) and impartial and disinterested, i.e., other to every other (like Sartre's series).

50 Rosa Luxemburg, 'The Junius Pamphlet' in M-A. Waters ed., *Rosa Luxemburg Speaks*, New York 1970, p. 269, and Rosa Luxemburg, *Selected Political Writings*, London 1972, p. 269.

51 PR, §303; CDR, p. 319; Luxemburg, 'Junius Pamphlet', p. 262.

5 Softening Up the State

1 For example, Gopal Balakrishnan, 'Future Unknown', *New Left Review* 32, 2005, pp. 5–21.

2   Chantal Mouffe, *On the Political*, London 2005, p. 7.

3   Niccolò Machiavelli, *The Discourses*, tr L. J. Walker, Harmondsworth 1970, p. 426 (3.8) and p. 154 (1.16); henceforth D.

4   D, p. 158 (1.17).

5   Ibid., pp. 386 (3.1), 162 (1.18) and 160 (1.17).

6   Ibid., p. 162 (1.18) cf the advice 'to live without factions, [and] to esteem the private less than the public good' in N. Machiavelli, *The Art of War* (1.33). In Machiavelli's time, 'corruption' had not acquired its modern association with pecuniary advantage.

7   D, pp. 360 (2.25) and 160 (1.17).

8   Niccolò Machiavelli, *The Florentine Histories*, tr C. E. Lester, New York 1845, 5.1; henceforth FH.

9   D, p. 159 (1.17).

10 Ibid., p. 159 (1.17).

11 Ibid., pp. 113–4 (1.4).

12 Livy, 2.32–3.

13 D, pp. 114–5 (1.4) and 123–4 (1.6).

14 Ibid., p. 119 (1.6).

15 Ibid., p. 121 (1.6).

16 Ibid.

17 FH, 3.5, cf. FH, 4.27.

18 Ibid., 3.1.

19 Ibid., 7.1.

20 Ibid., Prologue and 3.5.

21 D, p. 387 (3.1).

22 Ibid., p. 114 (1.4).

23 Ibid., pp. 112 (1.3) and 223 (1.46).

24 Ibid., pp. 116 (1.5) and 158 (1.17).

25 Ibid., p. 154 (1.16).

26 Ibid., pp. 153–4 (1.16).

27 Samuel Huntington, 'Political Development and Political Decay', *World Politics* 17, 1965, p. 386; *Political Order in Changing Societies*, New Haven 1968, (79) (47).

28 *Political Order*, p. 86.

29 'Political Development', pp. 408–9.

30 *Political Order*, 81; 'Political Development', pp. 411 and 409.

31 Gunnar Myrdal, 'The "Soft State" in Underdeveloped Countries' in P. Streeten ed., *Unfashionable Economics*, London 1970, p. 229.

32 Ibid., p. 233 (cf. G. Myrdal, *Asian Drama*, New York 1968, vol. 2, pp. 897–8).

33 Myrdal, 'Soft State', p. 235; Amartya Sen, 'Political Rights versus Economic Needs', Rothschild Foster Human Rights Trust Lecture, 1993, available at Rothschildfostertrust.com.

34 Joel Migdal, *Strong Societies and Weak States*, Princeton 1988, pp. 24–41.

35 See I. Ortiz, S. Burke, M. Berrada and H. Cortés, *World Protests 2006–2013*, Initiative for Policy Dialogue and Friedrich-Ebert-Stiftung Working Paper, New York 2013, and Samuel J. Brannen, Christian S. Haig and Katherine Schmidt, *The Age of Mass Protests: Understanding an Escalating Global Trend*, Center for Strategic and International Studies, Washington, DC 2020.

36 Wolfgang Streeck, 'The Crises of Democratic Capitalism', *New Left Review* 71, 2011, pp. 7, 29 and 28.

37 Karl Polanyi, *The Great Transformation*, 2nd ed. Boston 2001, pp. 196–7. The London riots of 2011, for example, coincided with FTSE 100 low for the entire year, Peter Atwater, *Moods and Markets*, London 2012, p. 48.

38 Philip Bobbitt, *The Shield of Achilles: War, Peace and the Course of History*, London 2003, p. 229.

39 Milton Friedman quoted in Andrew Gamble, 'The Free Economy and the Strong State: The Rise of the Social Market Economy', *The Socialist Register* 16, 1979, p. 8.

40 Wolfgang Streeck, *The Rise of the European Consolidation State*, MPIfG Discussion Paper 15/1, Cologne 2015, p. 25.

41 D, pp. 281–2 (2.3).

42 Ibid., p. 123 (1.6).

43 Ibid., pp. 360 (2.25) and 123 (1.6).

44 Ibid., p. 278 (2.2).

45 See Richard H. Adams, Jr and John Page, 'Do International Migration and Remittances Reduce Poverty in Developing Countries?', *World Development* 33, 2005, pp. 1645–69.

46 See Joseph Carens, *The Ethics of Immigration*, Oxford 2013. For the economic argument see Philippe Legrain, *Immigrants: Your Country*

Needs Them, Princeton 2007. Further information can be found at Open borders.info

47   Jonathan Crary, *24/7: Late Capitalism and the Ends of Sleep*, London 2013.

48   On basic income, see the resources at the Basic Income Earth Network site, Basicincome.org. Variations on the theme of freedom from work extend from Paul Lafargue's *The Right to be Lazy*, London 1883, to Nick Srnicek and Alex Williams, *Inventing the Future: Postcapitalism and a World without Work*, London 2015.

49   Alex Boso and Mihaela Vancea, 'Basic Income for Immigrants? The Pull Effect of Social Benefits on Migration', *Basic Income Studies* 7, 2012, pp. 1–24. The needs-blind distribution of grain raised similar issues in the Roman republic, see Alessandro Cristofori, 'Grain Distribution in Late Republican Rome' in H. Jensen ed., *The Welfare State: Past, Present, Future*, Pisa 2002, pp. 141–51.

50   Samuel Huntington, *Who Are We? The Challenges to America's National Identity*, New York 2004, and Christopher Caldwell, *Reflections on the Revolution in Europe*, London 2009.

51   See Guardian/LSE, *Reading the Riots: Investigating England's Summer of Disorder*, London 2011, and Olivier Roy, 'The Nature of the French Riots', 2005, available at Riotsfrance.ssrc.org.

52   Carew Boulding, *NGOs, Political Protest, and Civil Society*, Cambridge 2014, pp. 9–10.

53   Ibid., pp. 41 and 9.

6 Slack

1   L. Gregory Hines, 'The Myth of Idle Resources: A Reconsideration of the Concept of Nonuse in Conservation', *Transactions of the Eighteenth North American Wildlife Conference*, Washington, DC 1953, p. 28.

2   Ibid., p. 34.

3   Ibid., p. 32.

4   John Muir, *Nature Writings*, New York 1997, p. 387 (journal entry, July 24, 1869); 'The Hetch-Hetchy Valley', *Sierra Club Bulletin*, January 1908, p. 220.

5   See Robert W. Righter, *The Battle Over Hetch Hetchy: America's Most*

Controversial Dam and the Birth of Modern Environmentalism, New York 2005.

6   Gifford Pinchot, *The Fight for Conservation*, New York 1910, p. 17 and pp. 15–6.

7   'Address of Governor Pinchot on Conservation Day', *Forest Leaves* 20, 1926, pp. 177–8.

8   US Department of Agriculture Forest Service, *Forests and National Prosperity: A Reappraisal of the Forest Situation in the United States*, (Miscellaneous Publication 668) Washington, DC 1948, p. 4.

9   Temporary National Economic Committee, *Investigation of Concentration of Economic Power*, Washington, DC 1940, p. 178. Cf. H. C. Moser, *Idle Lands … Idle Men*, St Paul, MN 1938.

10 Stuart Chase, *Idle Men, Idle Money*, New York 1941, p. 194.

11 US Department of Agriculture Forest Service, *New Forest Frontiers: For Jobs, Permanent Community, a Stronger Nation*, (Miscellaneous Publication 414) Washington DC 1941, p. 44.

12 John Maynard Keynes, 'Some Economic Consequences of a Declining Population', *Eugenics Review* 29, 1937, p. 17.

13 Quoted in Paul W. Hirt, *A Conspiracy of Optimism: Management of the National Forests since World War Two*, Lincoln, NE 1994, p. 107.

14 Aldo Leopold, *A Sand County Almanac* [1949], New York 2001, pp. 186, 179.

15 William Hutt, *The Theory of Idle Resources*, London 1939, p. 9n.

16 Ibid., pp. 25 and 24.

17 Ibid., p. 31.

18 L. Gregory Hines, 'Wilderness Areas: An Extra Market Problem in Resource Allocation', *Land Economics* 27, 1951, pp. 310–11.

19 John Krutilla, 'Conservation Reconsidered', *American Economic Review* 57, 1967, p. 783.

20 Ibid., pp. 784–5; Hutt, *Idle Resources*, pp. 27–8.

21 Krutilla, 'Conservation Reconsidered', p. 780; Hutt, *Idle Resources*, p. 27.

22 For example, *The Magazine of Wall St and Business Analyst* 69, 1941, p. 474; See also Benjamin M. Anderson, *Economics and the Public Welfare*, Princeton, NJ 1949, pp. 490–1.

23 US Congress, House of Representatives, *National Defense Migration:*

Hearings Before the Select Committee Investigating National Defense Migration, Washington, DC 1942, p. 8505.

24 James Tobin and Murray Weidenbaum, eds, *Two Revolutions in Economic Policy: The First Economic Reports of Presidents Kennedy and Reagan*, Cambridge, MA 1988, p. 25.

25 Ibid., p. 139.

26 Ibid., p. 157.

27 Ibid., p. 52.

28 R. M. Cyert and James G. March, 'Organizational Factors in the Theory of Oligopoly', *Quarterly Journal of Economics* 70, 1956, pp. 46 and 53.

29 Ibid., p. 42.

30 Richard M. Cyert and James G. March, *A Behavioral Theory of the Firm*, Englewood Cliffs, NJ 1963, pp. 43–4.

31 For a summary, see Walter Y. Oi, 'Slack Capacity: Productive or Wasteful?', *American Economic Review* 71, 1981, pp. 64–9.

32 Ahmed Riahi-Belkaoui, *Organizational and Budgetary Slack*, Westport CT, 1994, p. 1.

33 Yuerui Wu, Chen Zhang and Yi Cui, 'A Study on the Influence of Organizational Slack on Firm Growth' in J. Luo, ed., *Affective Computing and Intelligent Interaction*, Berlin 2012, p. 420.

34 Toshihiko Kato, Masaru Karube and Tsuyoshi Numagami, 'Organizational Deadweight and the Internal Functioning of Japanese Firms', H. Itami et al., eds, *Dynamics of Knowledge, Corporate Systems and Innovation*, Berlin 2010, pp. 134–5.

35 Hines, 'The Myth of Idle Resources', p. 34.

36 Albert O. Hirschman, *Exit, Voice and Loyalty: Responses to Decline in Firms, Organizations and States*, Cambridge, MA 1970, pp. 14, 9, and 15. Although he tries to differentiate his account of slack from that used in Depression economics, he too first considered slack at the macroeconomic level in his work on development (p. 10).

37 Albert O. Hirschman, *A Propensity to Self-Subversion*, Cambridge, MA 1995, p. 5.

38 Ibid., p. 151.

39 Niccolò Machiavelli, 'The Art of War' in *The Chief Works*, tr A. H. Gilbert, Durham, NC 1958, p. 726 (translation modified); Cyert and March, 'Organizational Factors', p. 53.

40   Jeremy Adelman, *Worldly Philosopher: The Odyssey of Albert O. Hirschman*, Princeton, NJ 2013, pp. 489–91.

41   Niccolò Machiavelli, *The Discourses*, tr L. J. Walker, Harmondsworth 1970, p. 360 (2.25) and p. 123 (1.6).

42   Ibid., pp. 102–3 (1.1).

43   Hirschman, *Exit*, p. 6.

44   Ibid., p. 9.

45   Ibid., pp. 12–3.

46   Ibid., pp. 70–1.

47   Machiavelli, *Discourses*, p. 278 (2.2).

48   Niccolò Machiavelli, *The Prince*, tr G. Bull, London 1999, p. 20.

49   Machiavelli, *Discourses*, p. 389 (3.1).

50   Niccolò Machiavelli, *The Florentine Histories*, tr C. E. Lester, New York 1845, vol. 2, p. 6.

51   Albert O. Hirschman, *Shifting Involvements*, Princeton, NJ 1982.

52   Frank Kermode, 'Waiting for the End', in M. Bull, ed., *Apocalypse Theory and the Ends of the World*, Oxford 1995, p. 258.

53   W. B. Yeats quoted in A. Norman Jeffares, *A Commentary on the Collected Poems of W. B. Yeats*, Stanford, CA 1968, p. 210.

54   Ibid., p. 285.

55   On Joachim's theory of history see Marjorie Reeves, 'The Original-ity and Influence of Joachim of Fiore', *Traditio* 36, 1980, pp. 269–316, and B. McGinn, *The Calabrian Abbot: Joachim of Fiore in the History of Western Thought*, New York 1985.

56   J. G. A. Pocock, *The Machiavellian Moment: Florentine Political Thought and the Atlantic Republican Tradition*, 2nd ed., Princeton, NJ 2003, p. 113.

57   Marjorie Reeves, *The Influence of Prophecy in the Later Middle Ages*, Oxford 1969, p. 43; on Savonarola and Joachim see D. Weinstein, *Savon-arola and Florence: Prophecy and Patriotism in the Renaissance*, Princeton, NJ 1970.

58   Quoted in Maurizio Viroli, *Machiavelli's God*, Princeton, NJ 2010, p. 180.

59   However, Hirschman cannot have remained oblivious to the apocalyptic background after reading Pocock's *The Machiavellian Moment*, in which the interweaving of the discourses of apocalypse and corruption is a

significant theme. On Hirschman and Pocock, see Adelman, *Worldly Philosopher*, pp. 505–6, and 514.

60   For example, *The World's Work*, 59 (July 1930), p. 30.

61   Quoted in W. D. Klemperer, 'Is Idle Forest Land Always Economic Folly?', *Journal of Forestry* 67, 1969, p. 222.

62   Donald Worster, 'John Muir and the Roots of American Environmentalism' in *The Wealth of Nature*, New York 1993, pp. 182–202.

63   For example, Jeffrey E. Foos, *Beyond Environmentalism: A Philosophy of Nature*, Hoboken, NJ 2009, pp. 21–40.

64   See Reeves, 'Originality and Influence', pp. 290–1.

65   See Stephen Gardiner, *A Perfect Moral Storm: The Ethical Tragedy of Climate Change*, New York 2011, pp. 143–84.

7 Natural Cosmopolitanism

1   Aristotle, *Politics*, tr Harris Rackham, Cambridge, MA 1932, 1252b. (cf. 1253a2, 25). See further W. H. Ambler, 'Aristotle's Understanding of the Naturalness of the City', *The Review of Politics* 47, 1985, pp. 163–185.

2   Aristotle, *Politics*, 1253a.

3   Ibid., 1326a and b; Aristotle, *Nicomachean Ethics*, tr. Harris Rackham, Cambridge, MA 1926, 1170b31–33.

4   Aristotle, *Politics*, 1256b23–28.

5   Aristotle, *De Mundo*, 400b27.

6   Seneca, *De Otio*, 4.1 in A. A. Long and D. N. Sedley eds, *The Hellenistic Philosophers* [hereafter THP], vol. 1, Cambridge 1987, p. 431 (67 K).

7   Clement, *Strom.*, 4.26, quoted in Malcolm Schofield, *The Stoic Idea of the City*, Chicago 1999, p. 143.

8   For example, Philodemus, *On the Stoics*, 20.3–4: 'it is their [the Stoics' and Cynics'] view that we should not think any of the cities or laws we know of to be a city or law' (quoted in J. L. Moles, 'The Cynics and Politics' in A. Laks and M. Schofield, eds, *Justice and Generosity: Studies in Hellenistic Social and Political Philosophy*, Cambridge 1995, p. 133).

9   Plutarch, *De fortuna Alexandri*, 329a-b in THP, p. 429 (67 A).

10   For differing views on this see Malcolm Schofield, *The Stoic Idea of the City*, Chicago 1999, and Katja Maria Vogt, *Law, Reason, and the Cosmic City*, Oxford 2008, p. 62.

11   Julia Annas, *The Morality of Happiness*, New York 1993, pp. 263 and 265.

12   Diogenes Laertius, 7.85–6 in THP, p. 346 (57 A).

13   Cicero, *De finibus*, 3.62, THP p. 348 (57 F).

14   THP, p. 349 (57 G).

15   Annas, *Morality*, pp. 269–70.

16   Anonymous Commentator on Plato's Thaeatetus in THP, p. 350 (57 H).

17   Idem.

18   Diogenes Laertius, *Lives of the Eminent Philosophers*, tr R. Hicks, Cambridge, MA 1991, 2 vols [hereafter DL] 7.32–3.

19   Arius Didymus quoted in Schofield, *Stoic Idea*, p. 47 and Vogt, *Law*, p. 91.

20   Philodemus, *On Piety*, quoted in Schofield, *Stoic Idea*, pp. 74–5.

21   Heraclitus, *The Art and Thought of Heraclitus*, ed. C. H. Kahn, Cambridge 1979, § 83 (D53).

22   Ibid., § 81 (D.A 22) (cf. Homer, *Iliad*, 17.107); § 82 (D80); § 119 (D64).

23   Ibid., § 3 (D2).

24   Ibid., § 6 (D89).

25   Homer, *Iliad* 18.309.

26   Heraclitus § 89 (D21).

27   Sextus Empiricus, *Against the Logicians*, tr R. Betts, Cambridge 2005, p. 28 (129–31). Cf. Aristophanes, *Clouds*, 90: 'There dwell men who in speaking of the heavens persuade people that it is an oven, and that it encompasses us, and that we are the embers.'

28   DL, 7.32–34.

29   Ibid., 6.71.

30   Ibid., 6.63.

31   Ibid., 6.72. (Schofield, however, does not accept the latter saying as genuine, *Stoic Idea*, pp. 141–5.)

32   Epictetus, *Discourses*, III, 22,92; DL, 6.60.

33   See Schofield, *Stoic Idea*, pp. 50–1.

34   Immanuel Kant, *On History*, ed. L. W. Beck, New York 1963, p. 12.

35   Aristotle, *Politics*, 1253a.

36   Kant, *On History*, p. 105. See further Martha C. Nussbaum, 'Kant and Stoic Cosmopolitanism', *Journal of Political Philosophy* 5, 1997, pp. 1–25.

37   The affinity with Heraclitus is noted by L. W. Beck, *Commentary on Kant's Critique of Practical Reason*, Chicago 1960, p. 234. Kant quotes

Heraclitus's fragment on sleep (Kahn, *Heraclitus*, § 6 (D89)) in *Anthropology from a Pragmatic Point of View*, tr R. Louden, Cambridge 2006, p. 83.

38   Kant, *On History*, p. 111.

39   Immanuel Kant, *The Metaphysics of Morals*, tr M. Gregor, Cambridge 1996, p. 89.

40   Kant, *On History*, p. 15.

41   Ibid., p. 17.

42   Ibid., pp. 18–19.

43   Ibid., p. 20.

44   Ibid., p. 15.

45   Ibid., pp. 15–16.

46   Ibid., pp. 20–1.

47   Plutarch, *Moralia*, tr H. Cherniss, vol. 13, *Common Conceptions*, 1069.

48   Marcus Aurelius, *Meditations*, tr M. Staniforth, Harmondsworth 1964, p. 100 (6.42) (Heraclitus, § 91 (D75)).

49   Ibid., p. 45 (2.1).

50   Mandeville, *Fable*, p. 24.

51   Durkheim, *Division*, pp. 266–7.

52   HC, pp. 197 and 199.

53   Ibid., p. 199n.29 (Heraclitus, § 6 (D89); this is also the fragment quoted by Kant).

54   Ibid., p. 38.

55   Jonathan Crary, *24/7: Late Capitalism and the Ends of Sleep*, London 2013, p. 17.

Index